ON THE SIGNIFICANCE OF RELIGION FOR HUMAN RIGHTS

This progressive volume furthers the inter-religious, international, and interdisciplinary understanding of the role of religion in the area of human rights.

Building bridges between the often-separated spheres of academics, policymakers, and practitioners, it draws on the expertise of its authors alongside historical and contemporary examples of how religion's role in human rights manifests. At the core of the book are four case studies, dealing with Hinduism, Judaism, Christianity, and Islam. Authors from each religion show the positive potential that their faith and its respective traditions has for the promotion of human rights, while also addressing why and how it stands in the way of fulfilling this potential.

Addressed to policymakers, academics, and practitioners worldwide, this engaging and accessible volume provides pragmatic studies on how religious and secular actors can cooperate and contribute to policies that improve global human rights.

Pauline Kollontai is Professor Emerita in the Department of Religion, Politics and International Relations at York St John University, UK.

Friedrich Lohmann is Professor of Protestant Theology and Applied Ethics at the Bundeswehr University Munich, Germany.

Religion Matters:
On the Significance of Religion in Global Issues

Edited by Christine Schliesser, *Zurich University, Switzerland*
S. Ayse Kadayifci-Orellana, *Georgetown University, USA*
Pauline Kollontai, *York St. John University, UK.*

Policy makers, academics and practitioners worldwide are increasingly paying attention to the role of religion in global issues. This development is clearly noticeable in conflict resolution, development or climate change, to name just a few pressing issues of global relevance. Up to now, no book series has yet attempted to analyze the role of religion in current global issues in a coherent and systematic way that pertains to academics, policy makers and practitioners alike. The Sustainable Development Goals (SDGs) serve as a dynamic frame of reference. "Religion Matters" provides cutting edge scholarship in a concise format and accessible language, thereby addressing academics, practitioners and policy makers.

On the Significance of Religion in Conflict and Conflict Resolution
Christine Schliesser, S. Ayse Kadayifci-Orellana and Pauline Kollontai

On the Significance of Religion for Global Diplomacy
Philip McDonagh, Kishan Manocha, John Neary, and Lucia Vázquez Mendoza

On the Significance of Religion in Violence Against Women and Girls
Elisabet le Roux and Sandra Iman Pertek

On the Significance of Religion in Deliberative Democracy
Ruby Quantson Davis, Elizabeth Gish, Kudakwashe Chitsike

On the Significance of Religion for the SDGs
An Introduction
Christine Schliesser

On the Significance of Religion for Human Rights
Pauline Kollontai and Friedrich Lohmann

For more information about this series, please visit: www.routledge.com/religion/series/RELMAT

ON THE SIGNIFICANCE OF RELIGION FOR HUMAN RIGHTS

Pauline Kollontai and Friedrich Lohmann

With case study contributions by Hari Priya Pathak, Katajun Amirpur, and Ingrid Overbeck

Routledge
Taylor & Francis Group
LONDON AND NEW YORK

Designed cover image: Cover by Schwarzfalter GmbH
www.schwarzfalter.ch

First published 2023
by Routledge
4 Park Square, Milton Park, Abingdon, Oxon OX14 4RN

and by Routledge
605 Third Avenue, New York, NY 10158

Routledge is an imprint of the Taylor & Francis Group, an informa business

British Library Cataloguing-in-Publication Data
A catalogue record for this book is available from the British Library

ISBN: 978-1-032-38333-0 (hbk)
ISBN: 978-1-032-38334-7 (pbk)
ISBN: 978-1-003-34453-7 (ebk)

DOI: 10.4324/9781003344537

Typeset in Bembo
by Apex CoVantage, LLC

CONTENTS

NOTES ON THE AUTHORS

Pauline Kollontai is Professor Emerita in the Department of Religion, Politics and International Relations at York St John University, UK. Pauline's academic qualifications are in the disciplines of Peace Studies and Theology and Religious Studies. She combines these disciplines in her research, focusing on the overall theme of religion and society in various global contexts. This includes examining the role of faith-based actors; gender and peacebuilding; and religion, democracy and rights. Pauline is the author of several peer-reviewed articles, and chapters and has been co-editor for several books, the most recent being *Human Dignity, Human Rights, and Social Justice: A Chinese Interdisciplinary Dialogue with Global Perspective* (eds Zhibin Xie, Pauline Kollontai, and Sebastian Kim, 2020, Springer International). Pauline is the co-editor with Christine Schliesser and S. Ayse Kadayifci-Orellana of the Routledge series, *Religion Matters: On the Significance of Religion in Global Issues*. In 2019, Pauline was appointed as a member of the Resident Research Interdisciplinary and International Seminar Programme Team on "Religion and Violence" at the Centre of Theological Inquiry, Princeton.

Friedrich Lohmann is Professor of Protestant Theology and Applied Ethics at the Bundeswehr University Munich. He is also the chairperson of the Institutional Review Board of the same university, dealing with ethical questions of research. Working at the Department of Social Sciences and Public Affairs, his research and teaching try to bridge the gap between political and social sciences and theology. The main fields of his work are human rights and the ethics of peace and war. He regularly teaches a course on human rights together with a colleague from the Institute of Public and International Law of his department. One of his interests is the communication of scientific research to a broader public, for example as one of the editors of the journal *Zur Sache bw*, which is addressed to officers of the German army. He is the co-editor of the volume *Eine Theologie der Menschenrechte* (Springer VS 2019).

Contributing Case Study Authors

Katajun Amirpur has been Professor of Islamic Studies at the University of Cologne, Germany, since 2018. On April 1, 2022, she was appointed as Rector's Representative for the Critique of Racism at the University of Cologne. Katajun Amirpur studied Islamic studies and political science in Bonn and Theology in Tehran. From 2011 to 2018, she served as Professor of Islamic Studies at the University of Hamburg with a visiting professorship in 2014 at Dartmouth College. In addition to her academic work, Katajun Amirpur also appears as a committed political publicist, known to a wider audience for her books "Reform Islam" and the recently published biography on Khomeini. In 2016, she was awarded the Hamburg Teaching Prize for innovative teaching achievements, and in 2018 she was the recipient of the Tolerance Ring of the European Academy of Sciences and Arts. In November 2021, she was awarded the Reuchlin Prize of the City of Pforzheim.

Ingrid Overbeck is currently a research associate at the Institute of Languages and Cultures of the Islamic World at University of Cologne, Germany. Previously, she was a lecturer at Universities of Applied Sciences, at the Academy of Police in Hamburg and at bikup Cologne for inter-religious competencies. As a staff member of the Academy of World Religions/University of Hamburg, she has dealt in depth with representatives of the so-called Reform Islam and questions of intra-Islamic dialogue. Her special research interest is understanding the Muslim Principles of Nonviolence today; she is currently working on the consultation process "Religions, Diplomacy and Peace", a project of the Institute for Interdisciplinary Research at FEST, Heidelberg. Her other special research interest is Horizons and Fields of Spirituality in Shiite Islam. She has recently authored *09/11 und die Beziehungen zwischen den USA und Iran* (with Katajun Amirpur, Aus Politik und Zeitgeschichte 2021) and *Muslimische Frauenrechtlerinnen in Deutschland: ihre Diskurse, Handlungssphären, Organisationen und Akteurinnen* (Ergon 2020).

Hari Priya Pathak is an Assistant Professor in the Department of English, DSB Campus, Kumaun University, Nainital, India. Dr Pathak is a science graduate from Delhi University who later switched to humanities doing her post-graduate and research qualifications in English literature. She works in the areas of Feminist studies, mainly in relation to the Hindu religion, myths and women, Film studies, Cultural studies, translations, and other interdisciplinary fields. She has edited two prescribed textbooks as well as two English Grammar books for undergraduate study, published by Cambridge University Press. Her research papers and translations of some short stories from Hindi to English as well as some Kumaoni folksongs to English have been published in national and international journals.

ACKNOWLEDGEMENTS

The publication of this volume would not have been possible without the support of several persons and institutions. We'd like to thank, first of all, the contributing case study authors, Katajun Amirpur, Ingrid Overbeck, and Hari Priya Pathak, for adding perspectives from Islam and Hinduism. Both co-editors of the series "Religion Matters", Christine Schliesser and Ayse Kadayifci-Orellana, encouraged the project from the beginning and accepted to include the volume in the series. Additionally, Christine Schliesser helped us to find the right artwork for the book cover, and we thank the artists Manuel Dürr and Taco Hammacher for giving permission to reproduce one of their impressive art pieces on the cover. Thomas Frenz prepared the index of the book. The collaboration with the Routledge staff, especially Iman Hakimi, was excellent.

York and Munich, November 2022
Pauline Kollontai
Friedrich Lohmann

ABBREVIATIONS

BDFR	Beirut Declaration on Faith for Rights
BLHDL	Basic Law on Human Dignity and Liberty
BLM	Black Lives Matter
BTS	B'Tselem
BTYeb	Babylonian Talmud. *Tractate Yebamoth*.
BWC	Baptist World Congress
CDHRI	Cairo Declaration on Human Rights in Islam
DBM	Dalit Buddhist Movement
FBO	Faith–Based Organization
GE	*Gush Emunim*
ICLMWL	Islamic Council London and Muslim World League
IPIBA	Israel Population Immigration and Border Authority
LWF	Lutheran World Federation
MASI	Maha Association for Supporting Immigrants
MUHURI	Muslims for Human Rights
NGO	Non–Government Organization
OIC	Organization of Islamic Cooperation
PIL	Public Interest Litigation
PM	Prime Minister
RCC	Roman Catholic Church
RHR	Rabbis for Human Rights
ROC	Russian Orthodox Church
SAKD	South African Kairos Document
TM	Tag Meir
UDHR	Universal Declaration of Human Rights
UIDHR	Universal Islamic Declaration of Human Rights
UN	United Nations

UNDPI	United Nations Department of Public Information
UNGA	United Nations General Assembly
UNOHCHR	United Nations Human Rights Office of the High Commissioner
VDPA	Vienna Declaration and Programme of Action
VWCHR	Vienna World Conference on Human Rights
WARC	World Alliance of Reformed Churches
WCC	World Council of Churches
WPR	World Population Review

PART I
Summary

1

SUMMARY OF RECOMMENDATIONS FOR SECULAR AND RELIGIOUS ACTORS

Pauline Kollontai and Friedrich Lohmann

Introduction

Human rights are a core value enshrined and advocated through international law and to varying degrees in the laws of nation states. Developing and sustaining human rights as a standard that is advocated and adhered to from local through to international contexts is a task for secular actors and religious actors. Religion matters in human rights! It is, therefore, important to understand why, on the one hand, religion can oppose or be indifferent to human rights and why, on the other, religion can do the opposite and be an advocate for safeguarding human rights.

Recommendation 1: religious literacy for secular actors

Successful partnerships need a good understanding of each other. For secular actors, this means that religious literacy is important for their work with religious actors. It should be systematically available to a range of actors from community and local leaders to government leaders, regional, and international policymakers, and practitioners. Having a more critical and contextual knowledge and understanding of religion is an essential ingredient in engaging constructively with the complexities of religion, and in working towards ways in which religious actors can be regarded as equal partners.

Recommendation 2: "being equal partners" — organizational approach, principles, and values

Both secular and religious actors should aim to improve communication, build trust, and demonstrate respect towards each other as regards their faith or non-faith positions. As presented in the final chapter of this book, there is evidence showing

DOI: 10.4324/9781003344537-2

that over the past few decades there has been a concerted effort on the part of some secular actors in demonstrating and adopting these principles and values in their engagement with religious actors. Our second recommendation identifies three areas specifically for secular actors to improve on. These improvements we believe will show a more consistent and genuine interest in recognizing the importance of having religious actors involved in discussions and work because of the knowledge, insights, and experience religious actors can offer.

Recommendation 3: recognition of the legitimacy, influence, knowledge, understanding, and experience of the religious actor

Engaging with religious actors requires secular actors to adopt a recognition process that recognizes three key factors for this engagement. First, religious actors are seen by religious followers as having legitimacy in articulating and formulating values and concepts from religious teaching that influence and determine how people of faith live their daily lives in the private and public spheres. Second, the religious actor can be an influencer in reinforcing, challenging, modifying, or changing the opinions and actions of those within their faith communities. Third, religious actors can have "insider" knowledge and understanding that can assist secular actors in making decisions when designing and implementing policies and strategies.

Recommendation 4: religious actors promoting constructive partnership engagement and counteracting opposition within religions

Religious actors also have an important role in contributing to building these part-nerships and helping to overcome the scepticism that can exist among some secular actors. Such scepticism is normally based on the question of whether religion can make any valuable contribution to human rights work or because the words and actions (or inactions) of some religious actors demonstrate indifference or opposi-tion to human rights. Our recommendations to religious actors include asking them to consider if they can act responsibly and with integrity in the public sphere, practise transparency and respect in their work with secular actors, and take time to understand the perspectives of secular actors. Also, we recommend that religious actors need to continue to challenge, both privately and publicly, those within religions who either oppose or are indifferent to human rights.

PART II
Why Religion Matters

2

INTRODUCTION

Friedrich Lohmann and Pauline Kollontai

General introduction

"Imagine there's no heaven". It was in 1971, when John Lennon asked his audience to imagine a better, peaceful world of brothers and sisters. According to the song's lyrics, this would be a world without countries and possessions, and with "no religion, too". More than 50 years later, many will agree with Lennon, in saying that the religions of the world stand in the way of peace and of human development. Others will disagree and point out that religions, despite all conflict and oppression that have been justified in their name, have been important sources for human flourishing in past and present. Indeed, academic research likes to speak of "ambivalence" when it comes to the relevance of religion in social life. What was first coined for the relationship between religion and violence (Appleby 2000) can be said in a general manner: religion matters for human development and it matters in both directions, as a stopper and a catalyst.

But how does this "ambivalence of religion" shape out concretely? And what needs to be done in order to use the potentials of religion in a positive way? How can religious and secular actors cooperate and contribute to policies that make this world a better place? The present volume deals with these questions with regard to human rights. There is, indeed, a lot of ambivalence in the relationship between religion and human rights. In the struggle for global human rights, religions have been and continue to be both an obstacle and a driving factor. Religion matters for the global politics of human rights (Banchoff and Wuthnow 2011), be it on the macro level of governments and faith-based non-government organizations (NGOs) or on the grassroots level in which religious leaders of local communities play an important role. This has consequences for the way religion is perceived in academics and politics with regard to the implementation of human rights. Some see a religious foundation as a necessary pre-supposition for convincing rights talk,

DOI: 10.4324/9781003344537-4

while others contend that the global implementation of human rights would be easier without religion. Some see a concurrence between both, with human rights as "civil religion" taking the place of traditional religion (Porsdam 2012), while others argue that both can and should go hand in hand to foster human development for the better (Bucar and Barnett 2005). Not many would disagree that there is a need to reconcile religion and human rights (Salama and Wiener 2022).

The topic is too complex to deal with in a comprehensive manner within the two covers of a book. Many academic books have been devoted to the relationship between religion and human rights, and with a 400-page collection of 22 essays on the topic still calling itself an "introduction" (Witte and Green 2012), it would be presumptuous to pretend any comprehensiveness in a small volume of roughly 120 pages. In accordance with the general editorial principles of the series "Religion Matters", we therefore take a different approach. We zoom in on just four religions (Hinduism, Judaism, Christianity, and Islam), and we let adherents of these religions speak about what they perceive as problems and potentials for the idea of human rights within their own traditions. Once again, this does not pretend to be comprehensive, given the diversity each of these four religions contains in itself. We present case studies, not more. We hope, however, that the issues revealed and emphasized in these case studies have some exemplary value and that they allow better than any more comprehensive and "objective" approach to answer the three concrete questions raised above.

This introduction will give short summaries of the case studies. But before that, we must explain at least briefly how the two concepts of religion and human rights are understood in this volume.

Religion

The academic discussion about the concept of religion is as contentious as the one about its relationship to human rights. As in the first volume of this series (Schliesser et al. 2021: 12–13), we opt for a pragmatic approach to the question that departs from what usually is presupposed when a person or a community is called religious. Religion appears to be first and foremost a perspective, a way of seeing and interpreting oneself and the world. The specific feature, which distinguishes the religious perspective from others, is the assumption of a wider reality, beyond what is sensually perceivable, and the belief that this wider reality – the "transcendent" – is important for life. This defining aspect of being first and foremost a world view, a "web of interpretation", has been emphasized particularly by the anthropologist Clifford Geertz, following his observation of religious communities:

> The religious perspective differs from the common-sensical in that [. . .] it moves beyond the realities of everyday life to wider ones which correct and complete them, and its defining concern is not action upon those wider realities but acceptance of them, faith in them.

(Geertz 1973: 112)

Despite this emphasis on religion as a way of seeing (and not doing) things, Geertz does not neglect that the religious world view implies individual and collective practices (Geertz 1973: 125). This aspect of religion as a practice has been analysed, among others, by the sociologist of religion Martin Riesebrodt. "Religion is a complex of meaningful practices – that is, of actions – that are situated in a relatively systematic web of meaning" (Riesebrodt 2010: 72). The religious perspective does not only direct towards specific ritual practices. Furthermore, the believers receive from their world view orientation as to how to conduct life in general ("behavior-regulating practices", Riesebrodt 2010: 76), be it personal or social life. Therefore the strong ties between religion and ethics.

The religious world view tends to push believers towards forming communities which can over time become institutions with rather rigid rules and laws. It is, however, important to note that there are also non-institutional forms of religion. Way before the trend to a privatization of religion in modern Western societies (Luckmann 1967), there have always been mystics and prophets who live their religious lives in great independence from the mainstream of their respective faith tradition. With regard to human rights, it is, however, the institutional side of religion that is of the highest relevance.

Human rights

Even if some elements of human rights can be traced back to ancient times (Otto 1999; Sen 1997), the concept of *universal* human rights is tied to the attempt of the United Nations (UN) to establish a framework for global peaceful coexistence after the atrocities that had marked the first half of the twentieth century. The Universal Declaration of Human Rights (UDHR), as it was adopted in 1948 by the UN General Assembly (UNGA), claims in its preamble nothing less than to be "a common standard of achievement for all peoples and all nations", with the "recognition of the inherent dignity and of the equal and inalienable rights of all members of the human family" being "the foundation of freedom, justice and peace in the world". Three years before, the UN Charter already noted in its very first lines the determination of the signing governments "to reaffirm faith in fundamental human rights, in the dignity and worth of the human person, in the equal rights of men and women and of nations large and small".

Since then, human rights have been considered, together with peace, security, and development, to be the pillars of the UN, and the effort to guarantee equal rights for all human beings remains on top of the UN agenda way beyond its 75th anniversary (United Nations 2020). The UN 2030 Agenda for Sustainable Development emphasizes the implementation of human rights as necessary condition for global peace, security, and development:

> We reaffirm the importance of the Universal Declaration of Human Rights, as well as other international instruments relating to human rights and international law. We emphasize the responsibilities of all States, in conformity

with the Charter of the United Nations, to respect, protect and promote human rights and fundamental freedoms for all, without distinction of any kind as to race, colour, sex, language, religion, political or other opinion, national or social origin, property, birth, disability or other status.

(UN 2015: Declaration no. 19)

Among the 17 Sustainable Development Goals, which serve as the frame of reference for the book series "Religion Matters" and its effort to explore the significance of religion on global issues, questions of human rights are omnipresent. They are particularly addressed in goal no. 5 ("Achieve gender equality and empower all women and girls") and in goal no. 16 ("Promote peaceful and inclusive societies for sustainable development, provide access to justice for all and build effective, accountable and inclusive institutions at all levels").

Human rights are based on the idea that each human being has, due to their inherent dignity, rights that must be respected by all other human beings and especially government actors. The notion of "dignity" in the UDHR was chosen "in order to emphasize that every human being is worthy of respect" (Glendon 2002: 146). "Inherent" means, in this context, that there are no other conditions that must be fulfilled to share this dignity than being human. In the language of human rights declarations, this is often conveyed by saying that everyone is "born" with dignity and rights and that these dignity and rights are "inalienable". Given that everyone shares the same dignity, it follows that human rights are shared equally. It is against the idea of human rights that one person could have more rights than another one. Human rights are "equal" and "universal". However, it took some time to come to this conclusion. The Virginia Bill of Rights and other declarations from the eighteenth century, for example, have a blind spot with regard to slaves and women, and they proclaim validity only for the citizens of the respective state. The UDHR is the first declaration of human rights that is truly universal. It is a cornerstone of international law, leading directly to the International Covenant on Civil and Political Rights and the International Covenant on Economic, Social and Cultural Rights, both adopted by the UNGA in 1966 and since then ratified by an overwhelming majority of member states for which they represent binding law. In national law, many state constitutions contain constitutional rights that are inspired by the UDHR.

Human rights, their critics, and religion

Despite its frequent use in political declarations, constitutions, and international law, it would be premature to declare the concept of human rights as the uncontested leading norm of current politics. It can be argued that their success in the second half of the twentieth century was possible due to a unique window of opportunity (Moyn 2010). This window seems to close again in the first decades of the twenty-first century. The foundation of political rule in human rights was thought to prevent authoritarianism, and, therefore, it cannot be called a surprise that the current re-ascent of authoritarianism is connected to a strategy to put human rights aside. This strategy can build on criticisms that have accompanied the concept of human rights since its inception: human rights as opposed to order and security, creating chaos and useless deliberation where a strong hand is required; human rights politics as a utopia, conflicting with the true driving factor of politics, national interest; human rights as a solely Western concept, with its universal claims being colonialism in disguise; human rights individualism as forgetting about the importance of communities and loyalties for human flourishing; human rights as based on an erroneous vision of human freedom, suppressing moral responsibility and duties.

All these criticisms are nothing new. However, they shine in a new light when they are used by political leaders who want to get rid of human rights (and often also of international law) in order to cement their power. Given this situation of contestation, it is of particular importance to evaluate the relationship between religion(s) and human rights. Religious leaders exercise great moral and political authority in many regions of the globe. Their standpoint matters in the current struggle on human rights. The notion of an inherent human dignity is no stranger to religious thought, and there have been huge contributions from the world of religion to the progress of the human rights idea. But, as noted earlier, there is also a great religious reluctance when it comes to human rights. Actually, most of the mentioned criticisms are not least part of the vocabulary of religious and theological leaders.

So, we get back to the "ambivalence of religion" and the three questions behind this book: How does the "ambivalence of religion" shape out concretely with regard to human rights? What needs to be done in order to use the potentials of religion in favour of human rights? How can religious and secular actors cooperate and contribute to policies that make this world a better place?

Outline of this book

The case studies of this volume are divided in two in order to emphasize the ambivalence the respective religions express in human rights issues. The first half deals with examples that harbour problematic sides of religion, standing in the way of equal rights for all human beings. The case studies of the second half emphasize potentials of religion in support of human rights. Both series of case studies are headed by an orienting chapter that prepares the way by highlighting general aspects of religion that can explain its two faces with regard to human rights.

The case studies from Hinduism, Judaism, Christianity, and Islam, respectively, have a common thread. They show problematic and promising sides with regard to the same particular topic: women's rights in Hinduism, exclusionism and non-exclusivism towards Israel's non-Jewish citizens in contemporary Judaism, social change in Christianity, and an Islamic theology of human rights. By doing so, they emphasize the plurality of approaches and the margin of interpretation within the respective tradition. There is no monolithic position to women's rights in Hinduism and others. Within the same tradition, an identical issue can be dealt with in different ways, oscillating between full appreciation and hindrance of equal rights for all human beings. In the following overview, we give credit to this by summarizing both case studies from each tradition within the same paragraph.

Hari Priya Pathak focuses on women's rights in Hinduism. Women's lives in Hinduism are intricately bound with patriarchal social structures and various beliefs, superstitions, myths, customs, traditions, and other religious practices. The notion of "impurity" or "pollution" based on physical processes like menstruation, childbirth, and also widowhood leads to conditioned reflexes (psychological) and restricting women's space and other human rights. The first case study deals with the hindrances posed by Hinduism in imparting human rights to women.

Pathak's second case study shows the potentials within Hinduism to overcome these hindrances. Hindu scriptures like the Vedas, Upanishads, and Puranas depict women prominently in the form of powerful, benevolent, loving, and also aggressive goddesses and give primacy to the feminine principle *Prakriti*, without which the *Purusha* or the masculine is incomplete. In the Vedic period (1500 to 500 BCE) women had an honourable status. This situation, however, deteriorated with the changing sociopolitical scenario. After independence, several Women's Rights Organizations have been successful to procure several human rights denied to women as well as lower castes in India for a long time. This case study includes an examination of the Sabarimala case in India (2018), where the judiciary gave historic verdict by permitting women to enter the Sabarimala temple, upholding religious as well as constitutional rights of all citizens irrespective of gender.

Pauline Kollontai deals with attitudes within Judaism towards the rights of Israel's non-Jewish citizens. The first part of the case study draws on several Jewish thinkers who argue that biblical and classical Judaism does not contain the concept or language of human rights. This denial of the concept of human rights in the Jewish tradition is used by some contemporary Israeli religious Jews to justify their ideas and actions that deny and violate the rights of Israel's non-Jewish citizens. The case study focuses on *Gush Emunim*, the Jewish Orthodox settler movement organization, as an example.

However, there are other voices in contemporary Judaism than an exclusionist theology and praxis. The first part of the discussion in Kollontai's second case study focuses on Jewish teachings which enshrine concepts and values that support and promote the modern-day concept of human rights. Therefore, a case is made that Judaism can and does have a role in promoting and supporting human rights. The discussion moves on to look at how this is being manifested by the Jewish-founded religion-based organization *Tag Meir* (Light Tagging) in its work to help remove racism and violence in Israeli society and to remind the state's commitment that complete equality of social, political, and religious rights to all its inhabitants irrespective of religion, race, or sex will be ensured. Consideration of TM's work is also important to demonstrate the potential of Jews to reclaim and assert their prophetic heritage and teachings which combine to safeguard the existence and rights of all people.

A common problem many religions have with human rights is an attitude of glorifying the societal status quo as God-given. The social conservatism resulting from this is detrimental to human rights because their basic assumption of equal rights for everyone questions traditional hierarchies. Friedrich Lohmann's first case study gives two examples for this attitude from contemporary Christianity. The Russian Orthodox Church justifies patriotism from the God-given separation of humanity into nations. It also argues against gay rights and a full appreciation of women's rights from what is perceived as God-given human nature. Pentecostalism, on the other hand, is characterized by a strong belief in the presence of God's spirit in the world. In conjunction with a focus on salvation, this leads some currents of Pentecostalism into a social escapism that accepts and even sacralizes given societal hierarchies, at the expense of a full commitment to human rights.

There is, however, strong support for such a commitment in the Christian Gospel. In his second case study, Lohmann shows how a new reading of the life and preaching of Jesus is the driving force for several Christian theologies of liberation that engage in social activism and human rights advocacy. Latin American theology of liberation, the black theology in the United States, and the Christian Dalit theology in India are the examples this case study refers to in order to demonstrate the potential for a full embrace of the idea of human rights out of the heart of Christian belief, Christology.

Katajun Amirpur and Ingrid Overbeck delve with their case studies into the contested Islamic human rights discourse. Among Islamic theologians, there are different ideas of what human rights mean and, above all, how they are justified. The two case studies are devoted to the very contrasting positions on human rights, on the one hand, by the so-called traditional Islam, and, on the other, by the so-called reformist Islam.

According to the traditional Islamic view, human beings are given their rights by God. Rights are not given to people for their own sake but to fulfil their obligations towards God. This contention about the origin and purpose of moral precepts leads traditional Islamic theologians to a strong criticism of the secular idea of human rights, as is detailed by Amirpur and Overbeck in their first case study. For reformist Islam thinkers, on the other hand, the defence of human rights is reasonable and consistent with the Islamic precept of justice. In the second case study from within Islam, three post-revolutionary dissident key thinkers in political theology from Iran who are influencing public debates about human rights among Muslims worldwide will be introduced: Mohammed Shabestari, Abdulkarim Soroush, and Mohsen Kadivar. They represent the dialogue of Islamic thought with Western political philosophy, and the coming of age of the Islamic political theology reclaiming its pluralistic and democratic element. The case study unpacks these thinkers' views concerning human rights.

References

Appleby, R. Scott. (2000). *The Ambivalence of the Sacred: Religion, Violence and Reconciliation.* Lanham, MD: Rowman & Littlefield Publishers.

Banchoff, Thomas, and Robert Wuthnow (eds.). (2011). *Religion and the Global Politics of Human Rights.* Oxford/New York: Oxford University Press.

Bucar, Elizabeth M., and Barbra Barnett (eds.). (2005). *Does Human Rights Need God?* Grand Rapids, MI/Cambridge: Eerdmans.

Geertz, Clifford. (1973). "Religion as a Cultural System", in Clifford Geertz (ed.). *The Interpretation of Cultures: Selected Essays*. New York: Basic Books, 87–125.

Glendon, Mary Ann. (2002). *A World Made New: Eleanor Roosevelt and the Universal Declaration of Human Rights*. New York: Random House.

Luckmann, Thomas. (1967). *The Invisible Religion: The Transformation of Symbols in Industrial Society*. New York: Macmillan.

Moyn, Samuel. (2010). *The Last Utopia: Human Rights in History*. Cambridge, MA: Harvard University Press.

Otto, Eckart. (1999). "Human Rights: The Influence of the Hebrew Bible", *Journal of Northwest Semitic Languages* 25 (1): 1–20.

Porsdam, Helle (ed.). (2012). *Civil Religion, Human Rights and International Relations: Connecting People across Cultures and Traditions*. Cheltenham/Northampton, MA: Edward Elgar.

Riesebrodt, Martin. (2010). *The Promise of Salvation: A Theory of Religion*. Chicago, IL/London: The University of Chicago Press.

Salama, Ibrahim, and Michael Wiener. (2022). *Reconciling Religion and Human Rights: Faith in Multilateralism*. Cheltenham/Northampton, MA: Edward Elgar.

Schliesser, Christine, S. Ayse Kadayifci-Orellana, and Pauline Kollontai. (2021). *On the Significance of Religion in Conflict and Conflict Resolution*. London/New York: Routledge.

Sen, Amartya. (1997). *Human Rights and Asian Values*. New York: Carnegie Council on Ethics and International Affairs.

United Nations. (2015). *Transforming Our World: The 2030 Agenda for Sustainable Development*. Accessed from https://sdgs.un.org/sites/default/files/publications/21252030%20Agenda%20for%20Sustainable%20Development%20web.pdf [Date accessed November 13, 2022].

United Nations. (2020). *Declaration on the Commemoration of the Seventy-Fifth Anniversary of the United Nations*. Accessed from www.un.org/pga/74/wp-content/uploads/sites/99/2020/07/UN75-FINAL-DRAFT-DECLARATION.pdf [Date accessed November 13, 2022].

Witte, Jr., John, and M. Christian Green (eds.). (2012). *Religion and Human Rights: An Introduction*. Oxford/New York: Oxford University Press.

PART III

Religion and Human Rights

Problems

3.1

ORIENTATION

How and Why Religion Resists the Idea of Human Rights

Friedrich Lohmann and Pauline Kollontai

In 1832, Pope Gregory XVI issued an encyclical letter "On Liberalism and Religious Indifferentism". Reacting to a group from within the Church who asked for freedom of conscience, assembly, and the press, this encyclical was a fierce rebuke of the blossoming human rights movement. The Pope defended the existing alliance between throne and altar and condemned the efforts of "all those who struggle against this established order" (Gregory XVI 1832: no. 8). He was particularly straightforward against "the shameless lovers of liberty" (Gregory XVI 1832: no. 20):

> This shameful font of indifferentism gives rise to that absurd and erroneous proposition which claims that liberty of conscience must be maintained for everyone. It spreads ruin in sacred and civil affairs, though some repeat over and over again with the greatest impudence that some advantage accrues to religion from it. "But the death of the soul is worse than freedom of error," as Augustine was wont to say. When all restraints are removed by which men are kept on the narrow path of truth, their nature, which is already inclined to evil, propels them to ruin. Then truly "the bottomless pit" is open from which John saw smoke ascending which obscured the sun, and out of which locusts flew forth to devastate the earth. Thence comes transformation of minds, corruption of youths, contempt of sacred things and holy laws – in other words, a pestilence more deadly to the state than any other. Experience shows, even from earliest times, that cities renowned for wealth, dominion, and glory perished as a result of this single evil, namely immoderate freedom of opinion, license of free speech, and desire for novelty.
>
> (Gregory XVI 1832: no. 14)

Today, it would be difficult to find such a total rebuke of the idea of universal human rights issued by a religious leader. After being adopted by the United Nations

DOI: 10.4324/9781003344537-6

(UN) "as a common standard of achievement for all peoples and all nations" (UN 1948), human rights cannot be simply outlawed any longer. Religions have learnt to accommodate human rights. Even more, they discovered the potentials they have in their own tradition to embrace them (see Part IV of this book). Still, some reserves remain. Their main thrust joins the critique of political leaders, particularly from the Global South and East, stating that the universality of human rights must not rule out the value of existing moral traditions. We can take the words by the Iranian Deputy Foreign Minister at the Bangkok regional conference leading to the Vienna World Conference on Human Rights 1993 as an example:

> To enhance the universality of human rights and relevant instruments it is imperative to be cognisant of the cultural diversity of the human family and respect the values of various cultures. This would not only contribute to the richness of human rights norms, but also provide the best guarantee for their universal observance. The political predominance of one group of countries in international relations, which is temporary by nature and history, cannot provide a licence for imposition of a set of guidelines and norms for the behaviour of the entire international community, especially since these states do not present an ideal feasible or practical model, in theory or practice, nor do they possess admirable pasts.
>
> (quoted Boyle 1995: 87)

Following the claim that cultural diversity must be appreciated, religions and their leaders take the liberty to do their own reading of human rights, emphasizing some elements and criticizing others. This way of taking ownership of human rights is in itself legitimate – after all, cultural self-determination is itself a human right. However, it gets problematic when it is connected with a critical denial of the very core ideas of equal rights for everyone as the foundation of human flourishing. The case studies of this part of the book will elaborate on examples for that problematic endeavour to inhibit the full embrace of human rights on the grounds of religious belief systems. In the following, we give an overview of the roots for these religion-based reserves.

Traditionalism

A tradition is an idea or a practice that was transmitted (Latin: *tradere*) from the past and is valued positively by a group of human beings. It goes without saying that religions have a particularly positive view of their respective tradition because they usually honour persons of the past as exemplary figures, remember events of revelation, and often acknowledge sacred texts that have been passed over from previous generations of believers. They also have traditional practices of worship and adoration. Adherence to tradition becomes problematic – we call this traditionalism – when important distinctions within the respective tradition are not acknowledged. Such a distinction is, for example, the one within the Islamic legal tradition between *Shari'a*, the law revealed by Allah, and *fiqh*, the interpretation of *Shari'a* by medieval jurists.

> *Fiqh* is often mistakenly equated with *Shari'a*, not only in popular Muslim discourses but also by specialists and politicians, and often with ideological intent: that is, what Islamists and others commonly assert to be a "Shari'a mandate" (hence divine and infallible), is in fact the result of *fiqh*, juristic speculation and extrapolation (hence human and fallible).
>
> (Mir-Hosseini 2016: 34)

This missing distinction has immediate ramifications for the Islamic human rights discourse:

> In line with emerging feminist voices in Islam, I contend that pre-modern interpretations of the *Shari'a* can and must be challenged at the level of *fiqh*, which is nothing more than the human understanding of the divine will – what we are able to understand of the *Shari'a* in this world at the legal level. In other words, so-called "Islamic law" consists of "man-made" juristic con-structs, shaped by the social, cultural and political conditions within which Islam's sacred texts are understood and turned into law.
>
> (Mir-Hosseini 2016: 34)

Another failure of traditionalistic interpretations of religious texts is the missing distinction between the relevant message in the events that are narrated and the political and social conditions in which these events took place. There may have been a monarchy in place, and the social condition of women may have been one of subordination. It is, however, a mistake to take these conditions as God-given and unchangeable in the future. And, finally, religious traditionalism is also a prob-lem when pseudo-medical views from the past continue to haunt the present, as Hari Priya Pathak shows in her case study with regard to the alleged "impurity" of women in Hinduism.

Obligationism

Religious leaders frequently attack the central role of human freedom for the human rights idea. It is, they say, a mistake and, actually, a sin against God to speak primarily of human freedom and not of duties and obligations. The Universal Islamic Declara-tion of Human Rights (Islamic Council London and Muslim World League 1981), for example, affirms in its preamble "that by the terms of our primeval covenant with God our duties and obligations have priority over our rights". As Amirpur and Overbeck point out in their case study later in this book: "Human rights, according to the traditional Islamic view, are bestowed by God. Rights are not given to the human beings for their own sake, but to fulfil their obligations to God". An example for a similar position within Christianity is the "Basis of the Social Concept" of the

Russian Orthodox Church (ROC), which criticizes the liberal concept of human rights: "In the contemporary systematic understanding of civil human rights, man is treated not as the image of God, but as a self-sufficient and self-sufficing subject" (The Russian Orthodox Church 2000: IV.7; see Chapter 3.4).

It is true that the Universal Declaration of Human Rights speaks very little about duties and responsibilities, only in Art. 29. This deficit is criticized not only from the side of religion. In 1997, the InterAction Council, a group of elder statesmen from all over the globe, issued a "Universal Declaration of Human Responsibilities", with the aim to "complement the Human Rights Declaration and strengthen it and help lead to a better world" (InterAction Council 1997: Introductory Comment). Philosophical critics complain of the growing tendency to enforce personal interests in the name of human rights, going into the same direction as the ROC.

> In Western postmodern societies, the phrase "I have a right to X" is used interchangeably with the expressions "I desire or want X" or "X should be given to me". This linguistic inflation weakens the association of human right claims with significant human goods and undermines their position as central principles of political and legal organization.
>
> (Douzinas 2007: 12)

"It is the self-satisfied narcissism of the Enlightenment and human rights that is most in need of critique" (Stevenson 2017: 11).

However, if an abuse of the human rights idea is rightly criticized, it is a whole different story to claim a priority of obligations over rights. This last move, asked for by religious leaders, reverses the original thrust of the human rights idea. The claim for human rights was born and is revived again and again in situations of oppression, when rulers enjoy their liberties while asking their subjects to obey and fulfil their obligations. Even in democracies, majority rule can be implemented in a way that inhibits equal rights for everyone. The risk of abuse is far bigger when obligations are emphasized over rights than the other way around. One may also question whether religions, many of whom have a high esteem of human liberty, understanding themselves as practices of liberation of the self and underlining the connection between human dignity and freedom, are in a good position to assault the primacy of rights and liberties. There may be other than theological motives in play, as in Gregory XVI's encyclical, in which the exhortation to follow "the straight path" of obedience (Gregory XVI 1832: no. 17) was motivated not the least by an effort to "check the audacity of those who attempt to infringe upon the rights of this Holy See" (Gregory XVI 1832: no. 7). Asking for obedience is, after all, a well-proven way of rulers, be they political or religious leaders, to cement their power.

Collectivism

The call for more obligations and less rights is often connected with another critique of the human rights idea: its alleged (Western) individualism. The ROC's critique of the "self-sufficient and self-sufficing subject" is embedded in a social teaching that emphasizes the necessity of communities for human flourishing, not only the community of the Church but also – on the micro level – the family and – on the macro level – the Russian nation (see Lohmann's case study in chapter 3.4). Even stronger is the critique of human rights individualism coming from political rulers in Asia, like, for example, Singapore's long-time prime minister Lee Kuan Yew (Zakaria 1994), claiming "Asian values" that are mainly characterized by the subordination of the individual under collective loyalties, either in the family or in the nation. It is not sure at all whether this claim is in phase with the core messages of the main religions that are practised in Asia (Bloom et al. 1996), even if some Asian religious leaders are committed to it, like those embracing Hindu Nationalism (Juergensmeyer 1996). Another part of the world that can be mentioned here is Africa. The African Charter on Human and Peoples' Rights, also known as the Banjul Charter and adopted in 1981, is notorious for complementing individual rights by rights of collectivities (African Commission on Human and Peoples' Rights 1981).

> The African Charter treats a human being both as an individual and as a member of a collective (the "people"). [. . .] The communal aspect is emphasized in the rights guaranteed to "peoples" and in the recognition of the family as the "natural unit and basis of society".
>
> (Viljoen 2019: 205)

And, finally, voices from Latin America are leading in the request to include the community between human beings and the whole of nature into the human rights discourse (Fatheuer 2011). Both in Africa and Latin America, religious leaders embrace this more communitarian approach to human rights.

When evaluating these diverse impulses, it would be important to distinguish the different collectivities mentioned – the family, the Church, the nation, the people, nature – which cannot be done here. Suffice it to say that the critique of the "self-sufficient and self-sufficing subject" is something human rights advocates really have to think of. That is particularly true from a religious standpoint, given that religions are characterized by the notion of transcendence, as outlined in the introduction. Transcendence means interconnectedness, including at least some kind of dependency from others and surrounding nature. No surprise, then, that religious leaders are among those who ask not to forget the communal aspect of life in the human rights discourse.

Still, and in analogy to the issue of obligations and responsibilities dealt with in the previous section: if the well justified request for complementation is turned into a fundamental critique of the approach to human society from the individual and her or his rights (also rights towards the community!), it becomes problematic. Once again, this can be shown particularly from a religious standpoint. The notion of transcendence also means liberation from the dominant rules of society and its pathologies. After all, it is the individual and its dignity that lies at the heart of religion (Fuchs et al. 2019). The best proof for this statement may be the remembrance of those who have passed away, which is a central sphere of religious attention. We are far away from "Western" individualism when Gilgamesh bemoans the passing of his friend Enkidu (Mitchell 2014). The Dilmun Burial Mounds on the island of Bahrain, established around 2000 BCE, are a lasting testimonial for the high esteem of the individual human beings have kept in mind and religiously celebrated through the ages, with empires coming and going. It is, therefore, a problem and a kind of self-deception when religious leaders plead for a primacy of the collective over against the individual. Group rights are relevant, but, when overpushed, they become a problem because the labelling of human beings as members of group X and the accompanying tendency of "othering" stands in the way of peaceful interaction in society. The painful reconciliation process in Northern Ireland, with its insistence on communal rights, may be mentioned as an example (Curtis 2014).

Exclusivism

The notion of "othering" and its relation to a concept of human society, either nationally or globally, that is divided into collectivities leads us right away to the next problem that religions have and represent themselves for the human rights idea. Human rights begin at the individuals and their dignity, and they end up in a vision of humanity as a "human family" (UN 1948: Preamble) living together "in a spirit of brotherhood" (UN 1948: Art. 1). It is an important part of the ambivalence of religion with regard to human rights that they position themselves differently with regard to this vision. While there is a lot of potential in religion to fully embrace it (see Part IV of this book), religious actors often stand in its way by emphasizing the idea of "belonging", which then does not mean a belonging to the human family but first of all to the respective religion. It was this dividing element that John Lennon had in mind when he imagined a peaceful world without religion.

And there is, unfortunately, a lot of evidence to prove his reserves towards religion. Pauline Kollontai, in her following case study, gives a concrete example of exclusivism based on religious teaching in Judaism. On a global and policy-making level, the quest for religious freedom may be mentioned to show how religious exclusivism – which is, actually, a way to express a feeling of exceptionalism – haunts the current human rights discourse. Freedom of religion is a human right that is handily advocated even by religious actors who are rather reluctant to the idea of human rights in general. It is, then, understood as the freedom of members of the own religion abroad. This way of thinking freedom of religion becomes problematic – at the latest – when it is not accompanied by a spirit of brotherhood in the sense of granting freedom of religion also to those who practise another religion. Human rights are, after all, a reciprocal affair. Therefore, the critique of Arab leaders with regard to the religious freedom of Muslim minorities elsewhere on the globe would need to be backed by a particular welcoming attitude towards religious minorities in their own countries, which usually is not the case. Their advocacy of religious freedom seems to have an opportunistic, self-centred motivation. A lack of reciprocity in thinking of religious liberty is also a characteristic of Hindu Nationalism (Juergensmeyer 1996). Another example of religious exclusivism and exceptionalism is manifested by hardliners of the Christian right. "Christian nationalism demands Christianity be privileged by the State and implies that to be a good American, one must be Christian" (Baptist Joint Committee for Religious Liberty 2022).

Christian nationalism in the United States is attacked by a Christian human rights advocacy group:

> It often overlaps with and provides cover for white supremacy and racial subjugation. We reject this damaging political ideology and invite our Christian brothers and sisters to join us in opposing this threat to our faith and to our nation.
>
> (Ibid.)

It can, indeed, be argued that any kind of exceptionalism is a stranger to the notion of transcendence that is crucial for religious thinking. The belief in "wider realities" (Geertz 1973: 112) is rather opposed to sectarian feelings of superiority. William James famously associated religious experience with an "oceanic feeling" of universal embeddedness (Parsons 1998). This feeling implies an attitude of humility, tolerance, and solidarity and not one of exclusiveness, and it would be a mistake to identify the belonging to a religious community per se with exclusivism (Lohmann 2016). Nevertheless, this religious exclusivism does exist, at the expense of the human rights idea.

Escapism

The problems referred to in this chapter until now – traditionalism, obligationism, collectivism, and exclusivism – are manifested in the human rights discourse itself in the way religious actors take part in it. There is, however, another problem that religion can represent for the advocacy of human rights. We call it "escapism". By this we mean an attitude of religious believers and communities to take no interest in questions of society at all. This disinterest implies the acceptance of the societal status quo – which is a problem for the human rights idea with its interest in social change and human development.

Karl Marx famously called religion "the opium of the people". As a critical observer of society, he had well noted that religion, with its interest in the redemption of the soul and a future world to come, can lead to a sleepyheadedness with regard to the existing world and its inherent problems (the "can" is important here: Marx's thinking of religion is not only negative; see McKinnon 2005). There are enough examples, throughout the whole panoply of religions, of people who literally left their place in society for a remote, lonely hideaway in order to practise their belief undisturbed from earthly vanities. But Marx rather thought of those who remain full members of society and did not see the need for its change because of their religious preoccupations. Even worse: who sacralized the status quo by claiming its God-given nature. (There is a connection between religious traditionalism and escapism.)

There are examples of this kind of religious escapism still influencing politics and society. Lohmann, in his following case study, points out to some branches of Christian Pentecostalism. Their success in Africa and Latin America, often at the expense of liberation theology and its advocacy for human rights, is partly due to their way of establishing worship as a celebration of Christ's kingship and an asylum from the structural problems in the respective societies. One can also think of religions that favour contemplation like Buddhism, even if there are examples of an "engaged Buddhism" very open to the idea of human rights (see Chapter 4.1).

Conclusion

The attitude of escapism referred to in the end reminds us of the fact that religion can influence the evolution of human rights even without participating in it, which is another example for the different ways religion matters in society. The other attitudes of religious actors that were briefly analysed in this chapter – traditionalism, obligationism, collectivism, and exclusivism – are more straightforward contributions to the human rights discourse. As critical contributions, they ask partly valuable questions with regard to the need to complement the current human rights architecture. In their general direction, however, they tend to misunderstand the leading ideas of human rights and their closeness to the core values of religious thinking as a belief in "wider realities" (Geertz 1973: 112).

References

African Commission on Human and Peoples' Rights. (1981). *African Charter on Human and Peoples' Rights*. Accessed from www.achpr.org/legalinstruments/detail?id=49 [Date accessed November 13, 2022].

Baptist Joint Committee for Religious Liberty. (2022). *Christians against Christian Nationalism*. Accessed from www.christiansagainstchristiannationalism.org/statement [Date accessed November 13, 2022].

Bloom, Irene, J. Paul Martin, and Wayne L. Proudfoot (eds.). (1996). *Religious Diversity and Human Rights*. New York: Columbia University Press.

Boyle, Kevin. (1995). "Stock-taking on Human Rights: The World Conference on Human Rights, Vienna 1993", *Political Studies* 43: 79–95.

Curtis, Jennifer. (2014). *Human Rights as War by Other Means: Peace Politics in Northern Ireland*. Philadelphia, PA: University of Pennsylvania Press.

Douzinas, Costas. (2007). *Human Rights and Empire: The Political Philosophy of Cosmopolitanism*. Abingdon: Routledge.

Fatheuer, Thomas. (2011). *Buen Vivir: A Brief Introduction to Latin America's New Concepts for the Good Life and the Rights of Nature*. Berlin: Heinrich Böll Foundation.

Fuchs, Martin, Antje Linkenbach, Martin Mulsow, Bernd-Christian Otto, Rahul Bjørn Parson, and Jörg Rüpke (eds.). (2019). *Religious Individualisation: Historical Dimensions and Comparative Perspectives. Vol. 1.* Berlin and Boston: Walter de Gruyter GmbH.

Geertz, Clifford. (1973). "Religion as a Cultural System", in Clifford Geertz (ed.). *The Interpretation of Cultures: Selected Essays.* New York: Basic Books, 87–125.

Gregory XVI. (1832). *Mirari Vos – On Liberalism and Religious Indifferentism.* Accessed from www.papalencyclicals.net/greg16/g16mirar.htm [Date accessed November 13, 2022].

InterAction Council. (1997). *A Universal Declaration of Human Responsibilities.* Accessed from www.interactioncouncil.org/publications/universal-declaration-human-responsibilities [Date accessed November 13, 2022].

Islamic Council London and Muslim World League. (1981). *Universal Islamic Declaration of Human Rights.* Accessed from http://hrlibrary.umn.edu/instree/islamic_declaration_HR.html [Date accessed November 13, 2022].

Juergensmeyer, Mark. (1996). "Hindu Nationalism and Human Rights", in Irene Bloom, J. Paul Martin, and Wayne L. Proudfoot (eds.). *Religious Diversity and Human Rights.* New York: Columbia University Press, 243–261.

Lohmann, Friedrich. (2016). "Human Rights between Universalism and Religious Particularism", in Martin L. Pirner, Johannes Lähnemann, and Heiner Bielefeldt (eds.). *Human Rights and Religion in Educational Contexts.* Cham: Springer, 45–55.

McKinnon, Andrew M. (2005). "Reading 'Opium of the People': Expression, Protest and the Dialectics of Religion", *Critical Sociology* 31 (1–2): 15–38.

Mir-Hosseini, Ziba. (2016). "Human Rights and Islamic Legal Tradition: Prospects for an Overlapping Consensus", in Manfred L. Pirner, Johannes Lähnemann, and Heiner Bielefeldt (eds.). *Human Rights and Religion in Educational Contexts.* Cham: Springer, 31–43.

Mitchell, Stephen (ed.). (2014). *Gilgamesh.* London: Profile Books.

Parsons, William B. (1998). "The Oceanic Feeling Revisited", *The Journal of Religion* 78 (4): 501–523.

The Russian Orthodox Church. (2000). *The Basis of the Social Concept.* Accessed from https://old.mospat.ru/en/documents/social-concepts/ [Date accessed November 13, 2022].

Stevenson, Nick. (2017). *Human Rights and the Reinvention of Freedom.* London: Routledge.

United Nations. (1948). *Universal Declaration of Human Rights.* Accessed from www.ohchr.org/sites/default/files/UDHR/Documents/UDHR_Translations/eng.pdf [Date accessed November 13, 2022].

Viljoen, Frans. (2019). "Africa's Contribution to the Development of International Human Rights and Humanitarian Law", in Eunice N. Sahle (ed.). *Human Rights in Africa: Contemporary Debates and Struggles.* New York: Palgrave Macmillan, 203–229.

Zakaria, Fareed. (1994). "Culture is Destiny: A Conversation with Lee Kuan Yew", *Foreign Affairs* 73 (2): 109–126.

3.2

HINDU PERSPECTIVE

Human Rights of Women and the Notion of "Pollution" in Hinduism

Hari Priya Pathak

Introduction – woman's body as the site of "purity" and "pollution"

According to Harari, myths, stories, and fiction play a significant role in creating a society, because "believing in it enables us to cooperate effectively and forge a better society" (Harari 2014: 124). However, whether this creates a "better society" or not is debatable as it depends on who creates these myths and for whom. Further, these societies, says Harari, "are not always voluntary and seldom egalitarian", and "Most human cooperation networks have been geared towards oppression and exploitation" (ibid.: 116).

Several myths, beliefs, and superstitions originating from scriptures play an important role in governing our desires, attitudes, behaviour, decisions, actions, moralities, and practices in day-to-day life. These are deeply ingrained in our psyche and our identity is formed by them. According to Jung, the most important thing about myths is the psychology of their adherents. It is difficult to dissolve them as they belong to the reality of the psyche. "All myths emanate from the collective unconscious" (cited in Segal 1999: 81) but emphasizing too much on the unconscious is not wholly true, as "myths are consciously created, even if their creators are guided by the unconscious" (Segal 1999: 80). Malinowski claims that "myth expresses, enhances and codifies belief; safeguards and enforces morality, and vouches for the efficiency of ritual" (Malinowski 1948: 79).

Hindu society, which is bound by its caste system, is derived from the myth mentioned in the tenth book of the *Rig Veda*, the most ancient of the Hindu scriptures. This myth that Brahman created Brahmins, Kshatriyas, Vaishyas, and Shudras from his mouth, arms, thighs, and feet, respectively, later led to a strict division of society in creating categories where one caste (Brahmins) was on the highest pedestal and the other (Shudras) on the lowest, experiencing atrocities, exploitation,

DOI: 10.4324/9781003344537-7

and other sociopolitical discriminations. These categories were of divine origin and thus unquestionable, leading to the natural superiority of one caste over others, shaping their identity, psychology, and behaviour, resulting in internalization and at many times a resignation to the status quo.

This kind of internalization and resignation is visible among Hindu women too, because "Hinduism, as other religions, is a profoundly patriarchal, male-dominated religion in which women have been traditionally very subordinate, not enjoying the same rights and freedoms as men" (King 2004: 525). This, however, is in contradiction to the Hindu religious tradition where a woman is considered to be the source of power (*Shakti*). Hindu religious texts are full of ambivalence when it comes to women. It needs to be noted here that most of the sanctions towards women have been prescribed not in the *Vedas* or *Upanishads*, the two most ancient scriptures of the *Sanatan Dharma*, but in later texts like *Smritis, Epics*, and *Samhitas*. Wendy Doniger in her popular book, *On Hinduism*, writes: "*The Laws of Manu* deeply infiltrated Hindu culture, building into it many negative assumptions about the lower castes and about women that sharply restricted their freedom, regulated their behaviour and blocked their access to social or political power" (Doniger 2014: 268).

Widow burning (*sati*), which is now totally obsolete, was based on the scriptural belief that the wife of the deceased will reunite with her husband in the other world and would be deified here. There was a temptation of not only heaven but even renunciation. Widow remarriage was also not accepted in the Hindu religion, as a woman needed to atone for her husband's death, which somehow was the fault of her previous karmas. So, for this, she was to live a life of dejection with several religious injunctions imposed upon her.

A girl child is seldom welcome in a Hindu family, whereas the birth of a male child is rejoiced on because religion endows the male with the right to offer oblations to the manes and assist his parents to attain salvation (the ultimate goal of life in Hinduism). Moreover, a girl is to be married and given away with a dowry to another family. From the beginning, only her body and sexuality become the reason for her protection and restrictions. As soon as a girl reaches puberty, her menstruation becomes one more reason to confine her to a particular space. In Hinduism, "All margins . . . and matters issuing from them (peripheral extremities of the human body) are considered polluting . . . hair, nails . . . spittle, blood, semen, urine, faeces or even tears" (Murray 1994: 174), thus making menstruating women polluting and untouchable (like Shudras owing to their menial jobs). This is one of the reasons that a woman after childbirth is considered impure. This seclusion is not only physical but, in many ways, also psychological, where women internalize the belief about their own sexuality and body as polluting, just like Shudras internalized their inferiority. All this notion of women's subjugation arises from a very strong ideology formed by scriptures, structured, and propagated through patriarchal society. This chapter studies the notion of pollution and impurity of menstruating women in Hinduism, its mythic origin, and its serious implications for the human rights of women.

Menstruation myth

The myth of Indra slaying Vritra is mentioned in the *Rig Veda* more than a hundred times. This dramatic event has been interpreted by several historians and anthropologists in different ways. In the *Rig Veda*, Vritra is depicted as the withholder of the waters, the demon of droughts, a snake or dragon-like figure who dwells in the rivers or celestial waters or in a cavern in the earth (Chawla 1994: 2818). Several historians have likened Vritra to representing Indigenous people who were enslaved by the Aryans. Janet Chawla hypothesizes that "the figure of Vritra is inextricably linked with a pre-existing matristic social system and a world-view which valued the sacred and powerful feminine" (ibid.: 2818).

This myth of Indra slaying Vritra, who is a dragon, a serpent, or a formless being in the *Rig Veda* is in later scriptures like *Taittiriya Samhita* and *Vasishtha Dharmashastra* given the form of a Brahmin, a being of flesh and bones. In *Taittriya Samhita*, when Indra killed Vishwarupa or Trisira or Vritra:

> He seized with his hand the guilt of slaying him, and bore it for a year. Creatures called out upon him, "Thou art a Brahman slayer". He appealed to the earth, "Take a third part of my guilt". She said, "Let me choose a boon. I deem that I shall be overcome through digging. Let me not be overcome by that". He replied, "Before a year is out it will grow up for thee". Therefore before the year is out the dug-out portion of earth grows up again, for that was what she chose as a boon. She took a third of his guilt. That became a natural fissure; therefore one who has piled up a fire-altar and whose deity is faith should not choose a natural fissure, for that is the colour of guilt. He appealed to the trees, "Take a third part of my guilt". They said, "Let us choose a boon. We deem that we shall be overcome through pruning. Let us not be overcome by that". He replied, "From pruning shall more (shoots) spring up for you". Therefore from the pruning of trees more (shoots) spring up, for that was what they chose as a boon. They took a third part of his guilt, it became sap; therefore one should not partake of sap, for it is the colour of guilt. Or rather of the sap which is red or which comes from the pruning one should not partake [4], but of other sap at will. He appealed to a concourse of women, "Take the third of my guilt". They said, "Let us choose a boon; let us obtain offspring from after the menses; let us enjoy intercourse at will up to birth". Therefore women obtain offspring from after the menses, and enjoy intercourse at will up to birth, for that was what they chose as a boon. They took a third of his guilt, it became (a woman) with stained garments; therefore one should not converse with (a woman) with stained garments, one should not sit with her, nor eat her food, for she keeps emitting the colour of guilt.
>
> (*Taittiriya Sanhita*, Trans by Keith 1914: 107)

In later scriptures, the myth of Vritra again shows up as a Brahmin (Vritra was a formless being in earlier myth), whose killing makes Indra feel guilty and scared.

Brahminicide was the most heinous crime one could undertake, thus reserving hell for himself. He needs to be expiated, and it is the woman who shares the guilt of Indra becoming a partaker of the sin committed by Indra.

Scriptural injunctions on menstruating women

Thus, the menstrual flow is the guilt that keeps women impure, polluted, and untouchable for three to five days, and along with that come several religious injunctions. In *Taitriya Samhita* and *Vasishtha Dharamsutra*, it is mentioned clearly:

> A woman cannot act independently; she is under the authority of the man. "A woman who is neither a girl running naked nor in her menstrual period", it is stated, "is ambrosia".
> For month after month their menstrual flow washes away their sins. A menstruating woman remains impure for three days. She should not apply collyrium on her eyes or oil on her body, or bathe in water; she should sleep on the floor and not sleep during the day; she should not touch the fire, make a rope, brush her teeth, eat meat, or look at the planets; she should not laugh, do any work, or run; and she should drink out of a large pot or from her cupped hands or a copper vessel. . . . That guilt of killing a Brahmin manifests itself every month. Therefore, one should not eat the food of a menstruating woman, for such a woman has put on the aspect of the guilt of killing a Brahmin.'
>
> People in whose homes there are menstruating women, people who do not maintain the sacred fires, and people in whose family there hasn't been a vedic scholar – all these are equal to Sudras.
> (*Dharmasutras*, Trans by Olivelle 1999: 264–265)

In another *Dharamsutra*, one must clean oneself if touched by a corpse, a dog, or a woman who is menstruating:

> When a man touches an outcaste, a Chandala, a woman who has just given birth or is menstruating, a corpse, or someone who has touched any of these, he becomes purified by bathing with his clothes on; as also when he has gone behind a corpse or touched a dog.
> (*Dharmasutras*, Trans by Olivelle 1999: 103)

Implications

Patriarchy has taken menstruation as a reason to control women since the beginning, and myths and other beliefs have played a significant role in strengthening and making it a part of the social organization, moral order, and behavioural pattern for women. Malinowski states that "myths taken as a whole cannot be sober dispassionate history, since it is always made *ad hoc* to fulfil a certain sociological function, to glorify a certain group or to justify an anomalous status" (Malinowski 1948: 102).

Menstruating women are untouchable, impure, or polluted, and segregated for five days. They are confined to a limited space at home itself or sent out to a cowshed or huts in villages. The food is served to them either by slipping the plate under the door or given in such a way that the other person does not in any way touch them. If touched, the person is purified by sprinkling holy cow urine. In cities where the seclusion is liberal, they are prohibited to enter the kitchen or temple, or any other place of worship but can come out of this impurity and resume their ordinary chores on the fifth day after taking a head bath. This attitude not only instils inferiority but also humiliation and a sense of crippling helplessness among the womenfolk.

This idea that menstrual blood is abhorrent is strengthened through myths and other beliefs in several scriptures giving justification also for child marriage. A girl must be married after her third menstruation, or before even the menstruation begins. *Parashar Smriti* threatens dire consequences if the girl is not married according to the scriptural instructions. It states as follows:

> If a person does not give away a maiden when she has reached her twelfth year, his *pitrs* (ancestors) will have to drink every month her menstrual discharge. The parents and also the eldest brother go to hell on seeing an unmarried girl becoming Rajasvala.
>
> (Vaitheeswaran 2009: 5–7)

This passionate adoration for the religious conventions related to menstruation and restrictions is still prominent, especially in rural areas, in spite of widespread awareness brought about through science and technology, social media, and campaigns. These restrictions on menstruating women are not helping them but impeding their overall development and making them helpless.

Mobility and education for all are essential for the progress of a society or a nation. Menstruation has always been an obstruction to receiving education and has been actually taken as an excuse for depriving education to the girl child. In the Garhwal and Kumaon hills (situated in the West Central Himalayan region of Northern India), especially in the interiors, the taboo of menstruation is strong enough to prohibit the girl child to take the path to school which happens to be in the vicinity of the temple of a local god (which can be many and situated randomly in the hills). This alone can become a strong reason to deprive the girl child of her right to education, apart from many other reasons. Despite the government's several schemes to make education accessible to each and every one, religious and social stigmas related to menstruation hinder the speed or effect of these schemes when it comes to a girl child. The mobility of a girl child, which is a must to compete in today's world, is affected by menstruation and the restrictions posed by it.

Conclusion

Myths are dependent upon their interpretation for their meaning and thus the meaning may change according to who is the benefactor. They have a function to perform and can be taken as contextual. Menstrual segregation, which still persists, might have served an important purpose of cleanliness of water resources during ancient times when there was no provision of sanitary napkins and only scarce water resources. However, later it was conjoined and appropriated with several other beliefs depriving women of the human right of their full development and participation in public life. It played a significant role in restricting their productivity, due to early marriages, and inaccessibility to education and mobility, thus leading to their inferiority. A.S. Altekar, in his book *The Position of Women in Hindu Civilisation* (1938), shows clearly that the position of women is far better in a society with their role in production, access to education and public life than in a society confining and depriving them of education and public life through rules of pollution and purity. Unfortunately, many women seem to have internalized the idea of inferiority, physical or mental, propagated and appropriated by patriarchy over the ages through religion and traditional practices (Altekar 1938: 411–416).

However, with changing times, globalization, scientific innovations, and the rise of awareness about the role of religion concerning the position of women, several women rights organizations and non-governmental organizations like '*Durga Vahini*' and '*Guria India*' have already begun to oppose certain practices which degrade women's dignity as a human being. It was Gabriele Dietrich, an Indian activist, who pointed out the devastating effect of the Hindu religion on women's rights: "Religion has been one of the strongest forces in upholding the institution of the patriarchal family. Likewise, the patriarchal family has strengthened institutionalized religion" (Dietrich 1986: 159).

The need is to change with the changing times and evolving scientific knowledge to reinterpret the religious discourses in the view of acquired scientific knowledge. As Chris Weedon says, "we must think how our femininity and sexuality are defined for us and how we might begin to redefine them for ourselves" (Weedon 1987: 1). Redefining femininity and sexuality is possible by reinterpreting the religious myths in the light of rationality and then strengthen and reinforce these rational discourses through academics, media, films, documentaries, and other social platforms. There have been strong-minded women characters such as Draupadi, Kunti, Sita, and Keikeyi in the Hindu epics like the *Mahabharata* and *Ramayana*, who can be reinterpreted in the light of women's sexuality and empowerment (this is being promoted by contemporary writers like Amish Tripathi and Chitra Banerjee Divakaruni).

The roles of mothers become very significant here, who as women must create positive and rational attitudes towards natural events like menstruation. The taboos which inculcate inferiority of any kind must be discouraged by women themselves. Women in India have started taking cudgels against these age-old practices prohibiting them to enter a temple or any other worshipping place based on bodily taboos or sexuality. Menstruation taboos are gradually disappearing, especially in urban areas, thanks to globalization, development in science and technology, leading to mobility and rational thinking among people. Bollywood films by women directors like Deepa Mehta, Mira Nair, Shonali Bose, and Bishaka Datta have forced people to think about the irrationality and cruelty of certain customs, traditions, as well as taboos based on women's bodies, and sexuality and challenge gender and sexual stereotypes, which were very common in these films. Short documentaries like *Period. End of Sentence*, which won an Oscar in 2019, showed how a sanitary napkin "Fly" was produced by women in one of the villages in spite of the stigmas and taboos related to menstruation.

The Sabrimala case (2018) where there was a mass mobilization to enter the temple and worship Lord Ayappa, which disrupted the religious discourse on menstruation and also engaged the judiciary and all the major political parties, is one of the recent examples. It is a must to tell that it has long been the prerogative of only men to enter and worship Lord Ayappa and is prohibited for women between the ages of ten to fifty. This will be discussed in detail in Chapter 4.2.

References

Altekar, Anant Sadashiv. (1938). *The Position of Women in Hindu Civilization*. Banaras: The Culture Publication House, Banaras Hindu University.

Chawla, Janet. (1994). "Mythic Origins of Menstrual Taboo in Rig Veda", *Economic and Political Weekly* 29 (43): 2817–2827.

Dharmasutras The Law Codes of Ancient India. (1999). Translated and edited by Patrick Olivelle. New York: Oxford University Press.

Dietrich, Gabriel. (1986). "Women's Movement and Religion", *Economic and Political Weekly* 21 (4): 157–160.

Doniger, Wendy. (2014). *On Hinduism*. New York: Oxford University Press.

Harari, Yuval Noah. (2014). *Sapiens: A Brief History of Humankind*. London: Vintage Books.

King, Ursula. (2004). "Hinduism and Women: Uses and Abuses of Religious Freedom", in Tore Lindholm, W. Cole Durham, Bahia G. Tahzib-Lie, Elizabeth A. Sewell, and Lena Larsen (eds.). *Facilitating Freedom of Religion or Belief: A Deskbook*. Dordrecht: Springer. Accessed from www.researchgate.net/publication/312788997_Hinduism_and_Women_Uses_and_Abuses_of_Religious_Freedom [Date accessed January 21, 2022].

Malinowski, Bronislaw. (1948). *Magic, Science and Religion and Other Essays*. Glencoe, IL: The Free Press.

Murray, Milner Jr. (1994). *Status and Sacredness: A General Theory of Status Relations and an Analysis of Indian Culture*. Oxford: New York and Oxford University Press.

Segal, Robert. (1999). *Theorizing about Myth*. Amherst: University of Massachusetts Press.

Vaitheeswaran, B. (2009). *Parashar Smriti with English Translation*. Accessed from https://archive.org/details/ParasharaSmriti [Date accessed July 21, 2020].

The Veda of the Black Yajus School: Entitled Taittiriya Sanhita. (1914). Translated by Arthur Berriedale Keith. Cambridge, MA: Cambridge University Press.

Weedon, Chris. (1987). *Feminist Practice and Poststructuralist Theory*. Oxford: Blackwell Publishers.

3.3

JEWISH PERSPECTIVE

Jewish Exclusionist Theology in Israel

Pauline Kollontai

Introduction

This chapter focuses on how Judaism has been interpreted and used at times to passively resist or actively oppose the modern-day concept of human rights. The first part of the discussion examines how this is present among some contemporary academic thinkers. It then focuses on the Israeli settler movement organization, *Gush Emunim* (GE) (Bloc of the Faithful), which has promoted an exclusionist religious theology and considers three issues concerning this organization: (1) the theological basis and rationale of their belief and activities; (2) the nature and scope of their religious, social, and political influence and examples of their actions; and (3) the Israeli state's approach to settler violence in the context of extending the Judaization of Israel and the Occupied Territories.

"Judaism does not contain the concept of human rights"

Whether biblical and classical Judaism explicitly contains the language and concept of human rights is a disputed topic among scholars. Konvitz argues: "There is no word or phrase for human rights in the Hebrew Scriptures or in other ancient Jewish texts" (Konvitz 1972: 21). Borowitz writes: "The modern idea of human rights does not exist in that conceptualization in classic Jewish doctrine, for neither the Bible nor rabbinic literature speaks of human dignity in this way" (Borowitz 1990: 26). Henkin states: "Judaism knows no rights but duties, and at bottom, all duties are to God. Contemporary conceptions of human rights as political rights against human government was not central to original Judaism" (Henkin cited in Freund 1994: 51). Goitein argues that in much of medieval Rabbinic literature, the position was that "the basis of human rights was not egalite, for there prevailed a profound sense of the God-ordained natural inequality of men" (Goitein 1979: 33).

DOI: 10.4324/9781003344537-8

Religious justification and practices of the subjugation of Israel's non-Jewish citizens

Israel's Jewish Orthodox and Haredi religious establishments advocate specific interpretations of the sacred texts concerning God giving the ancient Israelites a "Promised Land" that articulates a disregard for non-Jews living in Israel (Genesis 15: 15–2; Joshua 1: 4–7). According to these interpretations, modern-day Israel is the new manifestation of this "Promised Land" and it must only be for Jews. Based on these interpretations, an argument is made for extending Israel's borders beyond "The Green Line", set out in the 1949 Armistice Agreement after the 1948 war between Israel and the surrounding Arab states of Egypt, Jordan, Lebanon, and Syria. Also promoted is the unequal treatment of Israel's non-Jewish citizens and the Palestinians living in the territories beyond "The Green Line" which Israel has occupied since 1967. This is justified by appealing to texts from the Books of Deuteronomy and Numbers where the ancient Israelites are commanded to occupy all of Canaan and preferably drive out the existing inhabitants (Deut. 20: 12–18; Num. 33: 50–53). In addition to these sacred texts, some within the Jewish Orthodox and Haredi religious establishments use one of the basic tenants of *Lurianic Kabbalah* (Jewish mysticism), which teaches that the Jewish soul and body are superior to the non-Jewish soul and body, and therefore the world was created solely for Jews, and the existence of non-Jews was subsidiary (Berg 1975).

Exclusionist religious theology: Gush Emunim and settler violence

The fundamentalist religious Zionist organization, GE was founded in 1974, propagating ideas and beliefs based on their "Greater Land of Israel" exclusionist theology. GE's theology is connected to aspects of the teachings of Rabbi Abraham Yitzhak HaKohen Kook (1865–1935), the first Ashkenazi chief rabbi of British Mandatory Palestine from 1904. Looking to the future realization of the re-establishment of a state of Israel, Kook saw religious Zionism as an essential platform for this realization and in ensuring that Israel would be "the foundation of God's throne in the world" (Kook OKIII 1938a: 191). Kook's view of an Israeli state was a religious messianic political entity where there would be no separation of religion and state. His political theology holds "tensions between two opposite poles: universalism and Jewish particularism" (Hellinger 2008: 534). The universalism aspect of Kook's thought is grounded in the theological teaching that each human being is made in the image of God. Thus, Kook states that "For only on the foundation of a soul that abounds in the love of humanity and love of every human being can the love of the nation transcend in its majestic nobility and its spiritual and practical greatness" (Kook OKIV 1938b: 405). The manifestation of these two competing aspects of Kook's work has been particularly visible in Israel after his teachings were resurrected and interpreted after his death by his son, Rabbi Tzvi Yehuda HaKohen Kook (1891–1982).

Like his father, Rabbi Tzvi Yehudah believed the state of Israel to be the contemporary manifestation of the biblical "Promised Land" bringing a long-awaited redemption for the Jewish people. However, unlike his father, who nowhere in his teachings advocates that a modern Israeli state is only for Jews or that non-Jews within its border should be subjugated to discrimination or violence, Rabbi Tzvi Yehudah consistently advocated the opposite and expressed a combative, aggressive, and intolerant religious theology towards those considered as the "other" or the "enemy" within Israel and surrounding territories. One key plank of Rabbi Tzvi Yehuda's teachings is complete Jewish sovereignty over all of Israel, which he argued was a fundamental precept of the *Torah*. He said this applied to the territory Israel was officially assigned under the 1947 UN Partition Plan for Palestine and the territories that Israel subsequently took in the Six-Day War of 1967. Speaking in 1974 at the *Merkaz HaRav Yeshiva* on Independence Day, Rabbi Tzvi Yehuda cited the biblical text from the Book of Numbers 33: 53: "And you shall dispossess the inhabitants of the land, and dwell in it. This requires that the land be clearly and decisively *kelal Yisraelit*, entirely in Jewish hands. As far as Judea, Samaria, and the Golan Heights are concerned, this shall not happen without a war! Over our dead bodies!" (Kook 1995: 25).

The Six-Day War in 1967 extended Israel's borders, taking the West Bank and East Jerusalem from Jordan, the Gaza Strip and the Sinai Peninsula from Egypt, and the Golan Heights from Syria. After the Six-Day War, Rabbi Tzvi Yehuda's ideas of Jewish redemption grew in influence in Israel among the right wing of the political and religious establishments and Jewish settler communities. Yehuda's students and followers believed that Israel's success in the Six-Day War was a sign that God was bringing about the redemption of Jews through human actions, and in 1974 the organization GE was established to assist with God's plan. GE advocated that Israel retain its occupation of the territories it had taken in 1967 by actively promoting and supporting Jewish settlement in these territories. GE had a significant ideological influence on the right wing of Israeli politics at national and local levels and infiltrated its ideas into some social and educational institutions (Zertal and Elder 2007; Newman 2013). Although GE has not functioned as a movement since the mid-1980s, its theological and ideological legacy remains present in the political, religious, and social discourses of Israeli society and has given birth to the settler movement. There have been many manifestations of GE's "Greater Land of Israel" ideology such as the settlers of *Gush Katif*, the *Yesha Rabbis Forum*, the political party *Kahane Chai*, and the *Hilltop Youth*.

GE has also helped create a culture of violence taken up by some members of Jewish settler communities through acts of vandalism, intimidation, and burning of non-Jewish homes and businesses. Rabbi Tzvi Yehuda's teaching that Jewish redemption was through the human action of settlement on the land provides justification for Jews to build their homes anywhere, even on territory that in the 1990s was given by the Israeli government over to the administration of the Palestinian Authorities. He argues that if the government of the day is not considered actively supporting Jewish settlement, the government is "illegitimate" claiming: "We are commanded by the *Torah*, not by the government. The *Torah* overrides the government, it is eternal, and this government is temporary and invalid" (Yehuda cited in Weissbrod 2013: 97). This claim has been used as a rationale for Jews taking the law into their own hands.

Growth of settler violence

GE's ideology of extremism and violence has been used to promote, justify, and support settler violence against Palestinians in all parts of the territories occupied by Israel and on occasions in Israeli towns where a majority of Israeli Arabs reside. Settler attacks on Palestinians in the Occupied Territories have grown particularly in number and frequency since 2009 (UNGA 2015; UNOCHA 2021). These attacks include physical violence towards Palestinian and Israeli Arabs; torching fields; destroying trees and crops; damaging homes, businesses, and other property; desecration or burning of mosques and churches; damaging other holy sites, and, in rare cases, homicide (Hareuveni 2021: 9).

A horrifying example of a Jewish settler attack occurred on July 31, 2015, when two Palestinian houses were firebombed in the early hours of the morning in the West Bank village of Duma. One of the houses was empty at the time, but in the other slept the Dawabsheh family. As a result of the firebombing, eighteen-month-old Ali Sa'ed Muhammad Dawabsheh was burned alive in the fire; both parents Sa'ed Muhammad Hassan Dawabsheh, aged 32, and Riham Hussein Hassan Dawabsheh, aged 26, died because of their injuries on September 7. The fourth member of the family, four-year-old Ahmad survived his injuries. In spring 2016, Amiram Ben-Uliel, aged 21, from Jerusalem, and a seventeen-year-old youth from the Samaria region identified as an accomplice were indicted on murder charges. After an intensive investigation, a senior Israeli Defence Force officer referred to the attack as "an act of Jewish terrorism" (Editor, (JTA) 2015: 1). Both men were given prison sentences. Also, in recent years, Palestinian farmers have been a particular target, being harassed and chased by settlers from their pasturelands, olive farms, and water sources. According to B'Tselem's latest report, from the beginning of 2020 to September 2021, there were 451 settler attacks; of these, 245 were directed explicitly at Palestinian farmers (Hareuveni 2021: 10). A recent example of this kind took place in September 2021 when several dozen Jewish settlers from the illegal Havat Maon and Avigavil settlements went to the small Palestinian village of Al Mufakara in the south Hebron hills. The settlers targeted a Palestinian shepherd throwing stones at him, stabbing his sheep, and killing six of them. In 2021, the Israeli Foreign Minister, Yair Lapid, publicly condemned the attack on Al Mufakara: "This violent incident is horrific, and it is terror. This isn't the Israeli way, and it isn't the Jewish way". The Health Minister Nitzan Horowitz said: "The violent rampage of lawbreakers is intolerable and we will stop it" (Boxerman and Spiro 2021: 1).

In the last half of 2021, settler attacks have continued in various places across Israel and in the Occupied Territories and significantly escalated in the West Bank

(Lynfield 2021). In November 2021, it was reported that the incumbent Israeli Prime Minister (PM) Naftali Bennett shared the expansionist views of the leaders of the settlers in expanding Israel's borders, "that Israel stretches to the river Jordan and he has promised to continue growing existing settlements" (Macintyre and Kierszenbaum 2021: 2). Of course, this does not necessarily mean that PM Bennett supported the use of violence by settlers but continuing to give official government support for the building of new Jewish settlements serves as a sign to many settlers that they should continue to assist the Israeli state by ensuring that Jews dominate the landscape of Israel proper, the Occupied Territories, and territories of the Palestinian Authority.

Those courageous Israeli Jews across all sectors of society who speak out against settler violence often face government criticism and sometimes become targets of settler extremism. The most recent example is that of the Public Security Minister Omer Bar-Lev, who, in a meeting on December 13, 2021 with the US Under-Secretary of State for Political Affairs, Victoria Nuland, told her: "Israel takes a severe view of settler violence" and he was working with the Defence Ministry to stop it. In response to Bar-Lev's comments, there were several social media messages from other government ministers who sought to discredit him. Interior Minister Ayelet Shaked tweeted: "You're confused, the settlers are the salt of the earth, the successors to the [early Zionist] pioneers", and Religious Services Minister Matan Kahana accused Bar-Lev of misrepresenting the truth about the settlers: "It's sad to see a person with such a rich, long security background accept such a false and distorted narrative" (Editor, (HRTZ) 2021). Bar-Lev was "reprimanded" by PM Bennett, who described the settlers as "the security wall for all of us" (Galon 2021: 1). Bezalel Smotrich, leader of the Religious Zionist Party, known as *Tkuma*, called Bar-Lev a "bastard", accusing him of being anti-Semitic and defaming the settlers and the blood they shed. He ended his tweet: "Shame on you, little man" (Breiner 2021: 1). As of December 27, Bar-Lev has been assigned 24-hour security because he has received threats on his life from Jewish extremists.

Israeli governments since 1967 have facilitated the building of 280 settlements in the West Bank, where over 440,000 settlers reside. Of these settlements, 138 were legally built and authorized by the state, and 150 are not officially recognized but most of these illegal settlements have been allowed to remain (Hareuveni 2021: 6). Only on two occasions have a very small number of settlements been officially removed by Israeli governments because of Israeli withdrawal from the Sinai in the early 1980s and then from Gaza and the northern part of the West Bank in 2005. According to Lein and Weizman, "Israeli governments have implemented a consistent and systematic policy intended to encourage Jewish citizens to migrate to the West Bank through significant government financial assistance and incentives" (Lein and Weizman 2002: 1). This policy has continued throughout the first part of the twenty-first century, and there has been no systematic action taken by Israeli governments to stop the building of illegal settlements.

Conclusion

GE and other Jewish religious extremist groups are motivated by a religious inter-pretation of Israel as a Jewish homeland, based on an exclusionist theology, fused with a xenophobic, zealous nationalism, where the rights of non-Jews are mini-mized, disregarded, and violated. The teachings of dignity, respect, and social jus-tice as espoused by the Hebrew prophets, a commitment given to these in the *1948 Founding Declaration of the Establishment of Israel*, are of little if any significance to such Jewish extremists. Unfortunately, this destructive religious zealotry, combined with the shift in Israeli politics in recent years to an illiberal democracy, only serves to increase tensions, violence, and insecurity for all Israelis. This situation will not bring about peace and justice for anyone when the rights of some are being limited and sacrificed. The question is, can Israeli Jewish voices promoting and attempt-ing to build Israel as an inclusive society succeed in their work by drawing on the teachings, principles, and values of Judaism and models of democracy? This ques-tion will be explored in Chapter 4.3, which looks at the work of *Tag Meir*, an Israeli Jewish faith-based organization.

References

Berg, Michael. (1975). *The Zohar*, with the Sulam Commentary. Jerusalem: Yeshivat Kol Yehuda.

Borowitz, Eugene B. (1990). "The Torah, Written and Oral, and Human Rights: Founda-tions and Deficiencies", in Hans Küng and Jürgen Moltmann (eds.). *The Ethics of World Religions and Human Rights*. London: SCM Press, 25–33.

Boxerman, Aaron, and Amy Spiro. (2021). "Police Arrest 3 Jewish Suspects in Attack on Palestinians in South Hebron Hills", *The Times of Israel*, September 29, 2021.

Breiner, Josh. (2021). "Bastard: Israeli Minister Faces Backlash for Vowing Action on Settler Violence", *Haaretz*, December 13, 2021.

Editor (HRTZ). (2021). "The One Thing Israel's Public Security Minister Got Wrong on Settler Violence", *Haaretz*, December 16, 2021.

Editor, (JTA). (2015). "Senior IDF Officer: Duma Attack was Definitely Jewish Terrorism", *Jewish Telegraphic Agency*, September 8, 2015.

Freund, Richard A. (1994). "Universal Rights in Biblical and Classical Judaism?", *Shofar: An Interdisciplinary Journal of Jewish Studies* 12 (2): 50–66.

Galon, Zehava. (2021). "The Settlers and Their Collaborators", *Haaretz*, December 23, 2021.

Goitein, Shlomo Dov. (1979). "Human Rights in Jewish Thought and Life in the Middle Ages", in David Sidorsky (ed.). *Essays on Human Rights: Contemporary Rights and Jewish Perspectives*. Philadelphia: The Jewish Publication Society of America, 247–264.

Hareuveni, Eyal. (2021). *State Business: Israel's Misappropriation of Land in the West Bank through Settler Violence*, Report of B'Tselem – The Israeli Information Centre for Human Rights. Jerusalem: B'Tselem Publications.

Hellinger, Moshe. (2008). "Political Theology in the Thought of Merka HaRav Yeshiva and its Profound Influence on Israeli Politics and Society Since 1967", *Politics, Religion and Ideology* 9 (4): 533–550.

Konvitz, Milton R. (1972). *Judaism and Human Rights*. New York: W. W. Norton.

Kook, Rabbi Abraham Isaac. (1938a). *Orot ha-Kodesh*, Vol. III. Jerusalem: Mosad Ha-Rav.

Kook, Rabbi Abraham Isaac. (1938b). *Orot ha-Kodesh*, Vol. IV. Jerusalem: Mosad Ha-Rav.

Kook, Rabbi Zvi Yehuda Hakohen. (1995). *Eretz-ha Zvi: ba-Ma'arakhah al Shlemut Arzeinu [On the Struggle over Greater Israel]*. Translated by Zalman Barukh Melamed. Beth-El: Netevei Or.

Lein, Yehezkel, and Eyal Weizman. (2002). *Land Grab: Israel's Settlement Policy in the West Bank*. Jerusalem: B'Tselem Publications.

Lynfield, Ben. (2021). "Israeli Settlers Escalate Violence in West Bank", *Foreign Policy Magazine*, November 9, 2021.

Macintyre, Donald, and Quique Kierszenbaum. (2021). "How Settler Violence is Fuelling West Bank Tension", *The Guardian*, November 28, 2021.

Newman, David. (2013). "Gush Emunim and the Settler Movement", in Joel Peters and David Newman (eds.). *The Routledge Handbook on the Israeli-Palestinian Conflict*. London: Routledge, 256–266.

United Nations General Assembly (UNGA). (2015). *Israeli Settlements in the Occupied Palestinian Territory, Including East Jerusalem, and the Occupied Syrian Golan*, Report of the Secretary-General to the General Assembly. New York: United Nations.

United Nations Office for the Coordination of Humanitarian Affairs (UNOCHA). (2021). *Protection of Civilians – Occupied Palestinian Territories*. New York: OCHA.

Weissbrod, Lily. (2013). *Israeli Identity: In Search of a Succession to the Pioneer, Tsabar, Settler*. Abingdon: Routledge.

Zertal, Idit, and Akivar Elder. (2007). *Lords of the Land: The War over Israel's Settlements in the Occupied Territories, 1967–2007*. New York: Nation Books.

3.4

CHRISTIAN PERSPECTIVE

The Appeal to Traditional Values as an Argument against Human Rights

Friedrich Lohmann

Introduction

Even if Christian churches and theology contributed a lot to the upcoming of a global human rights framework since the 1940s, building on a notion of human dignity that can be traced back to the Bible (Moyn 2015), the relationship between Christianity and the idea of human rights was and still is not without problems. The Amerindian genocide, the anti-democratic restoration in early-nineteenth-century Europe, and the Apartheid in South Africa are just three examples of flagrant human rights violations which had, at their time, support from Christian churches.

The long-standing reluctance to human rights within Christianity has various reasons. Some of it is purely opportunistic, given that the human rights revolution threatens established churches and their share of political power. When theology comes into play, two types of arguments can be distinguished: the claim for human rights can be opposed from a Christian standpoint either directly, as an infringement of the natural, God-given order, or indirectly, by stating that the struggle for political change in general is not the Christians' business.

"Natural order" as a roadblock in the way of human rights

The natural-order argument was put forward in an exemplary fashion already in the seventeenth century by Robert Filmer, in his critique of the republican ideas of Locke, Milton, and others. Filmer argued that hierarchical relationships are part of human nature and that there is theological legitimacy for monarchy by the analogy between a father as the head of a family, a supreme political ruler, and the God of Christian monotheism (Cuttica 2014). Filmer bolsters his point by Biblical

DOI: 10.4324/9781003344537-9

evidence, and indeed: references like Romans 13:1 ("Let every person be subject to the governing authorities; for there is no authority except from God, and those authorities that exist have been instituted by God" [New Revised Standard Version]) are prone to a rather anti-democratic reading. It is, however, obvious that Filmer doesn't manage convincingly to cope with the fundamental Christian belief that all human beings were created equal in dignity.

Even more obvious is the bias in the natural-order argument against human rights in the position which was taken at the time by the Dutch Reformed Church in South Africa in order to justify racial Apartheid: Biblical references speaking of the unity and community of all humankind are discarded, whereas the rather negligible verse Acts 17:26 is chosen to represent the hinge for a reading of the whole Scripture under the assumption of a God-established separation and hierarchy of races as part of the creation of humankind (Vosloo 2015).

Historically, the pitting of "natural order" against human rights in Christian theology gained momentum by the fact that the human rights movement in its early times was closely connected to political revolutions. The French Revolution in particular seemed to show to everyone that human rights were a bloody affair, sowing chaos, death, and anarchy instead of the good order. It was – and still is – a common accusation by Christian theologians and churches that the claim for human rights is the product of sinful hybris in those who don't want to accept the "natural" position given to them in society.

Human rights in the perspective of the Russian Orthodox Church

Next to the Bible, the doctrinal and moral tradition of the church can also be used as an instance to interpret the theologically required social order in the sense of the status quo. I will explain further the argumentative interplay between society, tradition, and nature as a problem for the human rights idea within Christianity by recurring to statements of the Russian Orthodox Church (ROC). "The Basis of the Social Concept" was adopted by the ROC in 2000, the "Basic Teaching on Human Dignity, Freedom and Rights" in 2008.

The ROC takes an ambiguous position with regard to human rights. It embraces them, but with an important disclaimer, as can be seen in the statement on "Human Dignity, Freedom and Rights":

> From the point of view of the Orthodox Church the political and legal institution of human rights can promote the good goals of protecting human dignity and contribute to the spiritual and ethical development of the personality. To make it possible the implementation of human rights should not come into conflict with God-established moral norms and traditional morality based on them. One's human rights cannot be set against the values and interests of one's homeland, community and family.
>
> (The Russian Orthodox Church 2008, III.5)

In this view, the natural order, represented by God-given moral norms and concretized in traditional values, is the critical measure that determines to which extent human rights are theologically justified or not. This is problematic because it sacralizes "the values and interests of one's homeland, community and family" without recognizing that these traditional values can easily be the product of a given culture, which may be driven rather by patriarchal or nationalistic ideas than by Christian morality.

A look into "The Basis of the Social Concept" (The Russian Orthodox Church 2000) offers some insight into the basic convictions that lead the ROC to this ambiguous approach to human rights. The document gives a comprehensive overview of the Church's positions to issues of social ethics, covering, among others, politics (including questions of war and peace), economics, and medicine. It is revealing that it starts – after some "basic theological provisions" – with reflections on the relationship between church and nation. While not neglecting the "universal nature of the Church" (II.2) and opposing "sinful phenomena as aggressive nationalism, xenophobia, national exclusiveness and inter-ethnic enmity" (II.4), the document subscribes to "national Christian cultures" (II.2) and "Christian patriotism" (II.3). The justification for this pro-patriotic standpoint is rather from the status quo ("Thus, the Orthodox Church, though universal, consists of many Autocephalous National Churches", II.2) than from the quoted Biblical evidence which underlines the one, universal church much more than its separation into national representatives.

The other social concept which is particularly emphasized in the document is the family:

> The role of family in the formation of the personality is exceptional; no other social institution can replace it. The erosion of family relations inevitably entails the deformation of the normal development of children and leaves a long, and to a certain extent indelible trace in them for life.

> (X.6; emphasis in the original)

There is a connection between family and nation as social realities: "The living continuity of generations, beginning in family, is continued in the love of the forefathers and fatherland, in the feeling of participation in history" (X.6). The reflections on family, gender, and sexuality use references from the Bible and the tradition of the Church but refer also to the created, natural order: "The difference between the sexes is a special gift of the Creator to human beings He created" (X.1); "*Holy Scriptures and the teaching of the Church unequivocally deplore homosexual relations*, seeing in them a vicious distortion of the God-created human nature" (XII.9; emphasis in the original). Empirical arguments are used as well: "'The change of sex' through hormonal impact and surgical operation has led in many cases not to the solution of psychological problems, but to their aggravation, causing a deep inner crisis" (XII.9). The argumentation with regard to the relationship between men and women – "fundamental equality", yet "natural distinction" with different "callings" – tries to navigate between modern achievements in the emancipation of women and a traditional, God-given ascription of roles:

> *While appreciating the social role of women and welcoming their political, cultural and social equality with men, the Church opposes the tendency to diminish the role of woman as wife and mother. The fundamental equality of the sexes does not annihilate the natural distinction between them, nor does it imply the identity of their callings in family and society.*
>
> (X.5; emphasis in the original)

The document adheres to the idea of human rights, "based on the biblical teaching on man as the image and likeness of God, as an ontologically free creature" (IV.6):

> The right to believe, to live, to have family is what protects the inherent foundations of human freedom from the arbitrary rule of outer forces. These internal rights are complimented with and ensured by other, external ones, such as the right to free movement, information, property, to its possession and disposition.
>
> (IV.7)

However, the claim of such rights is criticized when it allegedly loses connection with God's commandments and divine law: "In the contemporary systematic understanding of civil human rights, man is treated not as the image of God, but as a self-sufficient and self-sufficing subject" (IV.7). Given that human freedom is acknowledged further above, it is not clear from the outset at which point the "image of God" changes into "a self-sufficient and self-sufficing subject", or, in other words, which human rights claims are justified in the Church's interpretation and which are not.

The "Basic Teaching on Human Dignity, Freedom and Rights" also subordinates human rights to the (traditional) "norms of morality": "*The development and implementation of the human rights concept should be harmonized with the norms of morality, with the ethical principle laid down by God in human nature and discernable in the voice of conscience*" (III.3; emphasis in the original). The natural-order argument is taken up as well (e.g. I.4: "Sin overturns the hierarchy of relations in human nature").

This line of arguments in favour of "hypermasculinity" (Zorgdrager 2013) – with the two aspects of sexism at the expense of women emancipation and homophobia – is rooted in "the late Soviet conservative ethos" (Agadjanian 2017) and, much deeper, in an idea of the so-called Russian identity. At the same time, the ROC is an important "moral norm entrepreneur" (Stoeckl 2016), influencing current Russian society and politics. The following passage from Vladimir Putin's

Televised Address on Ukraine on February 24, 2022 sounds like taken directly from Patriarch Kirill's sermons:

> They [the West] sought to destroy our traditional values and force on us their false values that would erode us, our people from within, the attitudes they have been aggressively imposing on their countries, attitudes that are directly leading to degradation and degeneration, because they are contrary to human nature.
>
> (Putin 2022)

All in all, the evidence from statements of the ROC laid down in this chapter shows in exemplary fashion a problem many churches still have with human rights: they see that the Christian notion of an equal dignity of every human being implies human rights claims, but at the same time, they want to honour traditional moral norms from their cultural context, which leads to an ambiguous relationship of these churches to the human rights idea. The attempt to distinguish between justified and unjustified human rights claims by recurring to the God-given, created nature of humanity makes things worse because it presumes some theological justification for moral norms which are actually rooted in cultural history – like, for example, the degradation of transgender people – and not in the Christian understanding of humanity as a community of equals.

Human rights in the perspective of Pentecostalism

The theological arguments referred to up to now in this chapter have in common that they see a connection between Christian convictions and the concrete shape of politics and society. They argue against human rights because they assume that human rights stand in the way of the good, natural, and Christian order of society. A second type of problem for the human rights idea within Christianity is connected to theological assumptions that deny altogether that the quest for a better society is on the church's agenda. They emphasize the necessity of personal redemption and see the church as an institution of salvation without any bearing on questions of social ethics. Life here and now is dwarfed by the eternal life that awaits the pious soul. Morality is reduced to an individual struggle with sin, whereas political action is considered a mundane affair.

Such forms of escapism from society have a long history within Christianity. Examples can be found in monasticism, pietism, and Pentecostalism, even if these strands of Christianity are not against social activism per se. Let's have a closer look at the latter, because of its growing social and political influence.

As has been noted (Cartledge 2021), the current rise of Pentecostalism in the Global South, and its attractiveness particularly among the poor, can be explained by its offer of an alternative reality in worship and congregation: the experience of the Holy Spirit is believed to dignify someone independently of the social rank and, therefore, leads to an acceptance of the social and economic system as it is, without any incentive for a change of the status quo. No need to engage for a more human society because dignity, healing, redemption, and social recognition are offered by the Holy Spirit via the Church.

This conservative political stance has a second source, in addition to the spiritual escape option in the experience of worship. For Pentecostal faith, Jesus Christ, who already in his life on earth is believed to have been a powerful healer, has been governing the world since his ascension to heaven. Pentecostal hymns are full of praise for Christ, the king, who is in charge of the world. "Christ is the one who presently reigns" (Atkinson 2020: 218), which brings about a tendency in Pentecostalism to accept the status quo and to sacralize traditional moral norms.

On this ground, Pentecostal ethics with regard to human rights can get surprisingly close to the natural-order argument, which was presented and discussed earlier. A study from Brazil in which several Pentecostal leaders were asked about their opinion on human rights comes to the following conclusion:

> This leadership seeks to build bridges with the ideals of human rights, but often – and the clearest case in this regard is their position of defending the right to life – the source of inspiration is the Christian formulation of natural law of men.
>
> (Machado 2018: 117)

The problem is that this view of the natural law reinvigorates outdated scientific opinions, just because they fit with what is believed to be the Christian norm: "However, religious leaders tend to adopt those pseudo-scientific perspectives most closely related to their own positions when they are compelled by cultural changes around them to review their value systems" (Machado 2018: 114). Whereas freedom of religious expression is strongly supported by the Pentecostal leaders – which brings us back to the aforementioned opportunism, only this time not against but in favour of a specific human right – they tend to oppose women rights and gay rights. Traditional family values are the cornerstone of Pentecostal ethics, and if Pentecostal churches engage in politics, they do so in order to protect these values (Bartelink 2020).

This embrace of traditional norms is surprising if one takes into account that Pentecostalism is characterized by a high degree of dynamism, due to the belief in God's living spirit as the centre of its spirituality. It is stunning to see Pentecostal leaders, at least some of them – due to the inner dynamics of the Pentecostal movement, it is impossible to give any general assessment – recur to the notion of natural law in order to justify the primacy of the traditional family over the human rights movement. The explanation I would like to suggest is the Christ is King Christology mentioned earlier, in combination with a conservative social and political agenda: by claiming that Jesus Christ is the powerful ruler of the world, albeit still contested by sin and devil, Pentecostal Christians tend to sacralize or at least accept traditional moral values and hierarchies, at the expense of a full espousal of the human rights idea and its critical potential for social change. The embrace of the Prosperity Gospel – God's election of a person manifests itself through material success – by many neo-Pentecostals is another sign of this social conservatism.

The two examples from the ROC and Pentecostalism prove that traditionalism, as it was mentioned in Chapter 3.1, continues to stand in the way of a full commitment to human rights in Christianity. There are, however, strong theological arguments for such a commitment, as will be shown in the case study from Christianity in Chapter 4.4.

References

Agadjanian, Alexander. (2017). "Tradition, Morality and Community: Elaborating Orthodox Identity in Putin's Russia", *Religion, State and Society* 45 (1): 39–60.

Atkinson, William P. (2020). "Christology: Jesus and Others; Jesus and God", in Wolfgang Vondey (ed.). *The Routledge Handbook of Pentecostal Theology*. London/New York: Routledge, 216–225.

Bartelink, Brenda. (2020). "The Personal is Political: Pentecostal Approaches to Governance and Security", *The Review of Faith & International Affairs* 18 (3): 69–75.

Cartledge, Mark J. (2021). "'Liberation Theology Opted for the Poor, and the Poor Opted for [Neo-]Pentecostalism': Illustrating the Influence of the 'Prosperity Gospel' in Brazil", in Valburga Schmiedt Streck, Júlio Cézar Adam, and Cláudio Carvalhaes (eds.). *(De)coloniality and Religious Practices: Liberating Hope*. Fellbach: WiesingerMedia GmbH, 82–89. Accessed from https://iapt-cs.org/ojs/index.php/iaptcs/issue/view/39/IAPT.CS%20Vol%202%3A%20DeColonialityandReligiousPractices [Date accessed November 13, 2022].

Cuttica, Cesare. (2014). "Anti-republican Cries under Cromwell: The Vehement Attacks of Robert Filmer against Republican Practice and Republican Theory in the Early 1650s", in Dirk Wiemann and Gaby Mahlberg (eds.). *Perspectives on English Revolutionary Republicanism*. London: Routledge, 35–51.

Machado, Maria das Dores Campos. (2018). "Pentecostals and Human Rights Controversies in Brazil", *Religion and Gender* 8 (1): 102–119.

Moyn, Samuel. (2015). *Christian Human Rights*. Philadelphia, PA: University of Pennsylvania Press.

Putin, Vladimir. (2022). *Televised Address on Ukraine*. Accessed from www.bloomberg.com/news/articles/2022-02-24/full-transcript-vladimir-putin-s-televised-address-to-russia-on-ukraine-feb-24 [Date accessed November 13, 2022].

The Russian Orthodox Church. (2000). *The Basis of the Social Concept*. Accessed from https://old.mospat.ru/en/documents/social-concepts/ [Date accessed November 13, 2022].

The Russian Orthodox Church. (2008). *Basic Teaching on Human Dignity, Freedom and Rights*. Accessed from http://orthodoxrights.org/documents/russian-church-freedom-and-rights [Date accessed November 13, 2022].

Stoeckl, Kristina. (2016). "The Russian Orthodox Church as Moral Norm Entrepreneur", *Religion, State and Society* 44 (2): 132–151.

Vosloo, Robert R. (2015). "The Bible and the Justification of Apartheid in Reformed Circles in the 1940s in South Africa: Some Historical, Hermeneutical and Theological Remarks", *Stellenbosch Theological Journal* 1 (2): 195–215.

Zorgdrager, Heleen. (2013). "Homosexuality and Hypermasculinity in the Public Discourse of the Russian Orthodox Church: An Affect Theoretical Approach", *International Journal of Philosophy and Theology* 74 (3): 214–239.

3.5

ISLAMIC AND IRANIAN PERSPECTIVES ON HUMAN RIGHTS

Problems

Katajun Amirpur and Ingrid Overbeck

Introduction

Human rights as universal basic rights (Universal Declaration of Human Rights [UDHR]) to which every individual is entitled, regardless of ethnicity, origin, gender, and religion, have established themselves as a central topos in the West since 1948 and are understood as a universal minimum consensus of ethics.

At first glance, the function of human rights as a superordinate moral framework seems indisputable. At the same time, however, the limits of their normative claim arise from their specific political-legal character. Increasingly, the claim to the universality of human rights as formulated in the UDHR is criticized as being Western-centred. The dependence of human rights on a specifically Western context, which differs fundamentally from Islamic intellectual history, for example, is not sufficiently reflected, according to the critics. In addition, the insistence of Western states on human rights while simultaneously violating them, for example in international military conflicts, is perceived as a "double standard". A number of scholars argue that the view among Muslims that human rights and Islam are incompatible does not stem from opposition to the concept of human rights itself. Rather, they argue, it reflects a disenchantment and protest against Western hegemony and, consequently, against any ideology seemingly espoused by Western nations (Hakeem et al. 2012: 45–46).

The view of the Muslim public on human rights is characterized by different positions. Human rights are either seen as a purely Western concept, and often rejected as such, or interpreted as an authentic part of the Islamic tradition, or they are even reinterpreted as an Islamic "invention". In the so-called world religions, including Islam, there are points of contact with the idea of human rights, for example, in the concept of human dignity, which is protected in the Quran in verse 17:70: "We have honoured the children of Adam and carried them on

DOI: 10.4324/9781003344537-10

land and sea, and preferred them greatly over many of those We created". Or, as Prophet Mohammed said in his farewell sermon: "O people: your lives and your property, until the very day you meet your Lord, are as inviolable to each other as the inviolability of this day you are now in, and the month you are now in" (Al-Jahiz 1998: Kitāb al-Bayān wa-al-Tabyī). At the International Conference on Human Rights in Tehran in April 1969, religious figures also questioned the universality of human rights and stressed the need for their reformulation. In 1969, Iran played an active role in the establishment of the Organization of Islamic Cooperation (OIC), in which all Muslim-majority countries were represented. After the 1979 Islamic Revolution in Iran, the clergy increasingly questioned the legitimacy of universal human rights and advocated for the introduction of alternatives. In 1984, Sa'id Rajai-Khorasani, the United Nations (UN) representative of the Islamic Republic of Iran, described the UDHR as "a secular understanding of the Judeo-Christian tradition" (UN Doc A/C.3/39/SR.65, par 9: 1984). Other members of the OIC, including Saudi Arabia, Egypt, and Sudan, also rejected the concept of the universality of human rights, which led to the joint promulgation of an Islamic version of the Declaration of Human Rights, the "Cairo Declaration on Human Rights in Islam" (CDHRI) in 1990. This 1990 declaration was drafted after the first Universal Islamic Declaration of Human Rights of 1981 by the London-based Islamic Council, which is affiliated with the Muslim World League in Paris.

Is Universality of "human rights" a false path?

The Islamic human rights discourse has a completely different origin history and different determinants than the secular human rights discourse. The two questions of "origin" and "universality" are interlinked, because the demand and desire to make the acceptance of human rights concrete and effective depend not only on state enforceability but crucially also on people's identification so that they can be seen as an external expression of internalized values on what it means to be a human being. There are different ideas of what human rights mean and, above all, how they are justified.

The adoption of the Universal Declaration of Human Rights (UDHR) in 1948 was a response to the need to formulate a set of moral and legal criteria that could affirm the dignity and inviolability of the human individual, the emphasis being on human rights and freedoms. They were, at the same time, an appeal to the individual's capacity to act, independent of their political community. Human beings have their rights by virtue of being human. In the UDHR, human rights are, therefore, also assumed to exist. In this sense, the UN Charter speaks of "respect for human rights" (Art. 1) and the UDHR Preamble of "recognition of the inherent dignity and of the equal and inalienable rights of all members of the human family". Islamic thought, on the other hand, sees, first and foremost, the human being in the service of God and the community (Quran 3: 110), the constant point of reference and highest value in Islamic legal thought is the *umma*, the community of faith, or the collective of Muslims. It always involves a discourse on the rights of God and the rights of human beings, the former taking precedence over the latter (Arkoun 1994: 111). Human rights, according to the traditional Islamic view, are bestowed by God. Rights are not given to human beings for their own sake but to fulfil their obligations to God.

All sources of Islamic law, including the Quran, tradition, consensus, and *ijtihad*, are aimed at discovering and retelling the will of God. All of these sources originate from and are not independent of God's will. In this view, human rights must be perceived as a minor branch of "God's rights". Since in the Universal order, absolute sovereignty and omnipotence is only for God and all other powers are derived from him, God's right is the source and origin of all rights. It is disputed whether the interests of the human being were taken into account by God, since God can never be dependent on the interests of humans in his counsel, neither as a species nor as an individual (Nagel 2004: 130).

It was also the view of the founder of the Islamic Republic of Iran, Ruhollah Khomeini, whose position still dominates public discourse in Iran, that rights belong to God alone. The human beings have no rights but only duties towards God. It is possible for God or his representative on earth, the *valī-ye faqīh*, to grant humans certain rights, but since these are not inherent, they can be revoked at will by God or his representative. According to Khomeini, all people must subordinate their needs to the common good, the *umma*, and, therefore, cannot claim individual freedoms from the government (Khomeini 1971: Hokumat-e eslami). Formed in 2005, the Iranian judicial system has a special committee for human rights called the High Council for Human Rights. This committee is responsible for representing the Iranian government's position on human rights issues to the outside world. His secretary's position on human rights can be found in his treatise titled "Red Line of Freedom" (Larijani 2002: 33–57). His main argument is that freedom cannot be defined unconditionally without taking into account the human being's unity with God. In his view, the essence of human freedom is defined in relation to culture. This interpretation of freedom leads to human rights being dependent on culture.

The underpinnings of the conflict of traditional Islam with human rights

One of the best-known conservative clerics who participated in the discussion on human rights in Iran was Ayatollah Mesbah Yazdi (deceased January 1, 2021). Although Mesbah Yazdi was not involved in the drafting process of the CDHRI, his theories still play an important role in the discourses of conservatives in Iran on human rights today. Born in 1935, Mesbah Yazdi received his theological education in Qom, and his teachers were important Shiite figures such as Ayatollah Khomeini, Allameh Tabatabaei, and Ayatollah Behjat. After the revolution, he founded and directed the Imam Khomeini Research Institute and was a member of the Council of Experts on the Constitution from 1991 to 2016.

Yazdi rejects almost all the foundations of modern human rights, criticizing not only their theoretical and philosophical underpinnings but also their political implications. His view of Islamic human rights differs from the UDHR both thematically and substantively. In addressing the philosophical foundations of universal human rights, Yazdi followed the common reading after Mulla Sadra (1571–1631), according to which human beings essentially have no truly independent existence and thus no essential dignity or rights. Yazdi assumed the "oneness of being" and the absolute rule of God as well as the dependence of all other creatures on him. He also claims that Western secular principles cannot prove that human beings are entitled to rights. Western human rights, on the other hand, would put man in the place of God, so it is impossible to reconcile them with Islam, according to Yazdi:

> Western social thinkers and philosophers see human rights only in terms of individual and social rights, and therefore their efforts are focused on finding a way to resolve the conflict between individual and social rights. [. . .] But we believe in a third right based on our divine Islamic vision, which is even more important than the other two rights, and it is the right of the divine God [. . .]. The right of the divine God is for people to dedicate themselves to the path of perfection as described by God.
>
> (Yazdi 2009b: 35)

Western humanism gives the human being unconditional freedom that is incompatible with Islam:

> Religion in its essence – if we accept religion – means restriction of freedoms. Religion says you must have this belief, and that means I must not have any belief that I like [. . .]. The correct meaning of "no compulsion [*la ekrah*]" is indeed this.
>
> (Yazdi 2002: 13)

Yazdi believes that Islam is the top priority, not human beings or human rights, always mentioning "obligation" along with "rights". It is contrary to Islam to give priority to human rights, including the issue of equal rights for all people.

According to the traditional Islamic view, human beings are given their rights by God. Rights are not given to people for their own sake but to fulfil their obligations towards God. The Western term "right" in the sense of a guarantee without any consideration is not found in Islamic legal traditions. We find "*Huqūq al-Insān*", "*Huqūq-e-Bashar*", and "*Insāni Huqūq*" as translations of the term "human rights" into Arabic, Persian, and Urdu. *Haqq*, the singular of *Huqūq*, carries a rich history with an extensive meaning of "that which is established and cannot be denied", meaning "right" and "truth", also as a concept of "justice" and "that which is due". In the Quran, *Haqq* is used on numerous occasions to refer to "certainty", "reality", and "justice" and is both an attribute and a name of the Almighty. They serve as a means to realize broader societal interests and the common good (*maslahāh*).

This means that what is "due" and "just" can change depending on the situation. Critics argue that the notion of "due" and "just", when defined through the lens of patriarchy and power inequality, leads to violations of the rights of, for example, women and the marginalized.

Mesbah Yazdi criticizes different articles of the UDHR, yet to him, some rights such as equality, fraternity, non-discrimination, the right to freedom, and individual security mentioned in Articles 1–4 appear more like slogans. He believes that the rights mentioned in these articles cannot be proved by rational analysis independent from revelation, therefore discussing and determining such rights would require religious perspectives mentioned in Islamic law. In his discussion of the third article of the UDHR according to which "everyone has the right to life, liberty and security of person", Yazdi points out that, conceptually, the right to life is absolute and that, for example, no one shall be killed even if they committed a crime or offence. However, he claims that this absolute right is an illusion and that people who believe in the inviolable right to life do not believe in the right of God and only regard and define such laws based on the advantages and disadvantages that such laws might have on society (Yazdi 2009a: 87). According to Yazdi, the UDHR also has major structural flaws: lack of logical order, disregard for religion, inconsistency, lack of theoretical framework, neglect of the balance between rights and duties, and a lack of transparency (Yazdi 2009b: 11).

Very different opposing maxims

The very different opposing maxims in Islam on human rights are aptly described by Mohsen Kadivar. Kadivar, a trained Islamic jurist born in Shiraz in 1957, studied Islamic jurisprudence (*fiqh*) in Qom for 16 years and, in addition to the clerical rank of the *mujtahid*, he also holds a doctorate in philosophy. His criticism of the Iranian regime led to his imprisonment (1999–2000), the banning of his publications, and finally to his exile from Iran in 2008. He has been a research professor of Islamic Studies at Duke University since 2009. He illustrates the range of interpretations of Islam. Although many religious scholars have dealt with the matter of Islam and human rights for close to half a century in the Shiite Iranian context, Kadivar suggested that none of them squarely faced up to the challenge. They simply dismissed it by claiming (1) that the contents of human rights have all along been abundantly found in the religious texts (the Quran and the Sunna) and (2) that the notion of human rights in Islam is richer than the modern-day norms of human rights and that the Sacred Law giver has comprehensively enacted the "real rights of humans" (*ḥuqūq-i wāqiʿī-yi insān-hā*) within the *sharīʿa* precepts (Kadivar 2008: 118). Here, we are dealing with two different Islams, or rather, two interpretations. The so-called traditional or historical Islam is incompatible with human rights or democracy. Reformist Islam, on the other hand, which we call *eslâm-e nouandish*, is compatible with democracy. So what is the difference between the two? According to Kadivar, historical Islam, that is the traditional reading of Islam, is still the predominant interpretation among Islamic scholars. In Sunni Islam, it is represented by al-Azhar, an Islamic scholarly institution of international standing, based in Cairo and maintained by the Egyptian state. It includes, among others, Azhar University, the Academy of Islamic Studies, and the Azhar Mosque and is headed by an Islamic scholar, Sheikh al-Azhar. In Shia Islam, the theological schools of Najaf and Qom are the main proponents of this doctrine. Kadivar characterizes the most salient features of traditional and historical Islam as follows:

1   All religious rules and commandments found in the Quran are binding and unchanging over time. The same applies to most of the religious commandments from tradition. The jurists act as the guardians of Islamic law and the main interpreters of the religion.
2   The human intellect is not capable of grasping the intentions underlying the religious precepts. People's ignorance of the ultimate interests underlying these commandments means that the commandments themselves are also beyond human comprehension. Therefore, the believer must slavishly accept them even if they do not understand them. Changing or rejecting religious precepts on the basis of rational analysis is fundamentally unacceptable according to this interpretation. Nor can rational analysis be used to support them.
3   Although all people are absolutely equal in the world beyond and are judged there solely according to their piety, justice in this world is not the same as equality. Although Islamic law makes no legal distinction based on race or skin colour, it does make strict distinctions based on gender, religion, and individual freedom. Women often do not enjoy the same rights as men, non-Muslims not the same as Muslims.
4   Although it is not acceptable to force a Muslim to renounce their religion or to force a non-Muslim to accept Islam, changing religion is absolutely forbidden for Muslims. Apostasy is a crime and punishable. The ban on proselytizing Muslims and the punishment of apostasy show that there is no real freedom of religion in this system. The same applies to freedom of expression in general.
5   Important religious duties such as the commandment *al-amr bi-l-ma'rūf wa-n-nahy 'ani l-munkar* ("to enjoin the good and reject the bad"), and the call to *jihad* also enshrine a social responsibility for collective action and make indifference to the actions of others impossible. The religion sets Muslims the task of creating a "healthy" society and a healthy world. While this is to be done by peaceful means where possible, where positive change in others cannot be brought about by words alone, violence is permitted (Kadivar 2018: 25–26).

Differences in content between the UDHR and the traditional Islamic concepts of human rights exist above all in the area of equality rights. A fundamental element that is intrinsic to the universal human rights conventions is the equality of rights, which belong to the individual by virtue of their humanity and have a universal claim to validity. In Islam, the equality of believers before God is emphasized, but there are inequalities among different groups of people. Conflicts also arise when the individual sphere of rights is curtailed in favour of the common good.

Traditional Islam advocates the doctrine of the "equal worth" and "equal dignity" of the human person, rather than using the phrase "equality of men and women". In the area of women's human rights, they assume that women are permanently "protected" persons who are protected and preserved by men. This position leads to conceptually different norms such as "reciprocity" and "complementarity" between men and women. Human rights documents presented by Islamic platforms, including the OIC, therefore do not use the concept of "equality" in formulating human rights for women or use it in a strongly qualified sense, as the Arab Charter on Human Rights from 2004 in its Art. 3. Weighty counterarguments *for* the equality of the sexes can be found in the creation story of Islam with the first human couple and finally in the equal reward and punishment of both sexes in eschatology. "Mankind, fear your Lord, who created you of a single soul, and from it created its mate, and from the pair of them scattered abroad many men and women" (Quran 4: 1). Man and woman are partner beings according to the Quranic view. God created them from an essence or from a single living entity, a precursor of the sexes, so to speak.

Conclusion

Reformist Islam critiques traditional Islamic approaches to the question of compatibility between human rights and Islam and argues instead for their reconciliation from the perspective of a reformist Islam. In Chapter 4.5 three post-revolutionary dissident key thinkers in political theology from Iran who are influencing public debates about human rights among Muslims worldwide will be introduced.

References

Al-Jahiz in the *Kitāb al-Bayān wa-al-Tabyīn* presents this text of the Farewell Sermon, Al-Jāḥiẓ. (1998). البيان والتبيين/al-Bayān wa-al-tabyīn (in Arabic). Taḥqīq and sharḥ by 'Abd as-Salām Muḥammad Hārūn (7th ed.). al-Qāhirah: Maktabah al-Khānjī. 31–33, also mentioned in Musnad of Imam Ahmad (hadith no. 19774) as translated and annotated by Nuh Ha Mim Keller.

Arkoun, Mohammed. (1994). *Rethinking Islam: Common Questions, Uncommon Answers.* Boulder, CO: Westview Press.

Hakeem, Farrukh B., M.R. Haberfeld, and Arvind Verma. (2012). *Policing Muslim Communities: Comparative International Context.* New York: Springer.

Kadivar, Mohsen. (2008). *Ḥaqq al-Nās.* Tehran: Kabir, 118f.

Kadivar, Mohsen. (2018). "Islam and Democracy. Perspectives from Reformist and Traditional Islam", in John L. Esposito, Lily Zubaidah Rahim, and Naser Ghobadzadeh (eds.). *The Politics of Islamism. Diverging Visions and Trajectories.* Cham: Palgrave Macmillan, 25–26.

Khomeini, Ruhollah. (1971). *Hokumat-e eslami* (Der islamische Staat). o.O.

Larijani, Mohammad Javad. (2002). "Khatte qermez-e azadi", *Andisheh-ye Hawzah* 37: 33–57.

Nagel, Tilman. (2004). "Erst der Muslim ist ein freier Mensch!", in Georg Nolte and Hans-Ludwig Schreiber (eds.). *Der Mensch und seine Rechte.* Göttingen: Wallstein, 121–136.

United Nations (UN). (1984). Summary Record of the 65th Meeting, UN General GAOR, 3rd Comm., 39th sess, 65th mtg, UN Doc A/C.3/39/SR.65, 91–95 (7 December 1984).

Yazdi, Mesbah. (2002). *Dīn va Azadī* (Religion and Freedom). Qom: Imam Khomeini Institute.

Yazdi, Mesbah. (2009a). *Negahi Gozara be Hoquq-e Bashar az Didgah-e Eslam* (A Brief Look on Human Rights in Islamic Perspective). Qom: Moaseseye Pazhouheshiye Emam Khomeini.

Yazdi, Mesbah. (2009b). *Nazariyeye hūqūqiye eslām* (Legal Theory of Islam). Qom: Imam Khomeini Institute.

All verses of the Quran quoted here are drawn from A.J. Arberry. (1955). *The Koran Interpreted*. New York: Macmillan.

PART IV

Religion and Human Rights

Potentials

4.1

ORIENTATION

How Religion Can Contribute
to Human Rights

Pauline Kollontai and Friedrich Lohmann

Introduction

Research shows that religion can be a constructive player in promoting and actively supporting human rights. This chapter discusses religion's constructive resources, approaches, and mechanisms that can contribute to human rights work. The first section provides a general orientation into the topic by exploring the beginning of international human rights law and the religious connection. The following sections present an overview of examples of various religions that have been engaging with human rights theoretically and practically over the past few decades.

The evolution of international human rights law and the religious connection

Following the devastating events of World War II, the United Nations (UN) established a Commission in early 1947 on Human Rights, with Eleanor Roosevelt (First lady of the United States from 1933 to 1945) as chairperson because of her extensive advocacy work on civil rights. In December 1948, the Commission's draft of the Universal Declaration of Human Rights (UDHR) was officially accepted by the General Assembly of the United Nations (Glendon 2001). The concept and understanding of modern-day human rights and the foundation of international human rights law are found in this Declaration. These rights are proclaimed as inherent to all human beings as individuals, irrespective of nationality, place of residence, sex, national or ethnic origin, race, religion, language, or any other status. The UDHR states that "it is the duty of States to promote and protect all human rights and fundamental freedoms, regardless of their political, economic, and cultural systems" (UNGA 1948: 1). But state responsibility is the macro level of operation. Promoting and protecting human rights and holding governments

DOI: 10.4324/9781003344537-12

accountable for safeguarding these rights must also be the responsibility of groups, organizations, and individuals across the multifaceted levels of society. The Declaration contains 30 articles identifying a range of rights that include the right to life, liberty, and security; freedom of expression and assembly; freedom of thought, conscience, and religion; the right to housing, education, and work; freedom from slavery and torture; and the right to a standard of living adequate for the health and well-being of individuals and their family. The concept and practice of "Duties" are the focus of Article 29 "Everyone has duties to the community in which alone the free and full development of his personality is possible" (ibid.: 5). The UDHR is in its 74th year at the time of writing this book, and it has been translated into over 520 languages.

The Commission had representatives "from countries with majoritarian Atheist, Buddhist, Christian, Confucian, Hindu, and Muslim populations" (Witte and Green 2011: 7). It was also assisted by consultants and representatives from specialized agencies and non-governmental organizations (NGOs). Some of these were faith-based, such as the International Federation of Christian Trade Unions, the Commission of the Churches on International Affairs, the Consultative Council of Jewish Organizations, the Catholic International Union for Social Service, and the International Union of Catholic Women's Leagues (UNDPI 1949: 574). The Declaration drafting committee consisted of nine individuals, of which three individuals were identified as having a religious affiliation. Judge René Cassin, a Jewish jurist from France; Mr Peng-chun Chang from China, a distinguished Confucian scholar, educator, and diplomat; and Dr Charles Habib Malik, a theologian and philosopher, and a Maronite Christian originally from Lebanon. The input of these individuals was not intended for the Declaration to be grounded in any religious tradition or to present human rights as being of divine origin. Instead, it was intended to provide insights into how the concept of human rights was understood in various religious and cultural contexts. For example, Mr Peng-chun Chang is reported "to explain the Chinese concept of human rights to the other delegates and creatively resolved many stalemates in the negotiation process by employing aspects of Confucian doctrine to reach compromises between conflicting ideological factions" (UNGA 1948: 1).

Since 1948 other pieces of international human rights law have been established and ratified by the UN, these include the *International Covenant on Civil and Political Rights* (1966), *International Covenant on Economic, Social and Cultural Rights* (1966), *Convention on the Elimination of all Forms of Discrimination Against Women* (1979), *Convention of the Rights on the Child* (1984), *International Convention on the Protection of the Rights of all Migrant Workers and Member of their Families* (1990) and the *Convention on the Rights of Persons with Disabilities* (2006).

Also pertinent to the evolution of human rights is the Vienna World Conference on Human Rights (VWCHR) held in 1993, initiated by the UN, which brought together representatives from 171 states and 841 NGOs, including the involvement of several faith-based organizations. Initially, the Conference agenda was intended to focus predominantly on improving human rights mechanisms and processes; however, it became predominantly focused on questioning and examining the basic principles of universal human rights. The shift in the agenda's focus is said to have been the result "of the deep uncertainties, confusion and regional tensions that replaced the Cold War in international relations" and the serious increase, since the end of the 1980s, in the ethno-nationalist conflicts, within and between states in parts of Europe, Africa, and Asia and the resulting violation of human rights (Boyle 1995: 80). The VWCHR is said to have provided less in terms of offering immediate answers to the violation of human rights arising from ethno-nationalist conflicts, but it did produce the Vienna Declaration and Programme of Action (VDPA) which reaffirms the UN commitment to human rights, the need for relevant international law, and the responsibility of nation states and NGOs to be actively promoting and advocating human rights. The Preamble to the VDPA recognizes and affirms "that all human rights derive from the dignity and worth inherent in the human person, and that the human person is the central subject of human rights and fundamental freedoms" (UNHROHC 1993: 1). Article 1 states: "The universal nature of these rights and freedoms is beyond question. Human rights and fundamental freedoms are the birthright of all human beings; their protection and promotion is the first responsibility of Governments" (ibid.: 2).

Religions engaging practically with human rights

Since the early part of the twentieth century, most religions have begun to increase their consideration of the relationship between centuries-old teachings, traditions, practices, and contemporary human rights. According to Witte and Green, this is taking place "in Christian, Islamic, Judaic, Buddhist, Confucian, Hindu, and Indigenous communities alike" and includes both seeing how religion can nurture and support human rights and in challenging contemporary human rights (Witte and Green 2011: 19). Scholars and practitioners of religions differ on the degree to which the concepts and language of modern-day rights are present in the centuries-old sacred texts and teachings. But the growth of religious groups specifically identifying their work as related to human rights would suggest that they are finding concepts within their religious teachings and traditions and applying them to their own geopolitical and historical contextual reality. Some of this work is illustrated in the case studies presented in this chapter, but a brief mention of examples of other religious groups provides a sense of the global religious engagement with human rights work.

In India, during the 1950s, the Dalit Buddhist Movement (DBM) was founded by Dr Bhimrao Ramji Ambedkar to challenge the caste system and promote the rights of the Dalit community. He had expressed his concern before the founding of the DBM. In 1927, at the Mahad Conference, he said: "We want equal rights in society. We will achieve them as far as possible while remaining within the Hindu fold or, if necessary, by kicking away this worthless Hindu identity" (cited in Jaffrelot 2005: 119). Another example from the Hindu tradition is the organization Sadhana, founded in 2011, whose work is "driven by the values of social justice at the heart of our faith". Sadhana aims to "empower Hindu American communities to live out the values of their faith through service, community transformation, and targeted advocacy work", concerning various social justice issues including racial and economic justice, gender equity, and immigrant rights (Sadhana n.d.: 1). Since the 1980s, in South Korea examples include the Buddhist Human Rights Committee, the Buddhist Commission for the Protection of Human Rights of Foreign Workers, the Maha Migrant Assistant Group Council, and the Maha Association for Supporting Immigrants (MASI). All these Korean organizations have provided educational, medical, welfare and social support, and cultural activities to Korea's migrant communities. The MASI has been especially prominent in protecting the human rights and interests of female migrants and in working to empower immigrant-rights activists (Kim and Park 2020: 6). In Myanmar, Buddhist monks, students, and laypeople have held vigils and protests since the 1980s, demanding democracy and human rights from their military rulers.

In Afghanistan, the withdrawal of US and UK forces in August 2021 and the return of the Taliban to power has meant a serious deterioration of the rights of women in terms of access to all levels of education, the right to employment, and the reimposition of demanding that women must wear *hijab* and be accompanied by a male member of their family when out in public. Afghan Muslim women activists have been increasing their protests and demonstrations in Kabul demanding rights to education and employment and against the *hijab* directive, chanting "equality and justice", with their banners reading "Women's Rights, Human Rights". In late January 2022, Monisa Mubariz, co-founder of the Afghan Powerful Women's Movement, outlined the situation: "Women have been deprived of the right to work and participate in political and economic life. They are consistently repressed, punished illegally, insulted, and humiliated" (Zucchino and Akbary 2022: 3). Protesting for women's rights against the Taliban's interpretation of Islam's teachings on the role and status of women in the public sphere is a hazardous one. Still, Mubariz and other Muslim women are determined to show that within Islam, there are teachings that promote rights and dignity for women. In Kenya, the organization Muslims for Human Rights (MUHURI) was founded in 1997. Five core values guide the work of MUHURI: "transparency and accountability; gender parity and de-marginalization; respect for human rights; fairness and equity; and constitutionalism and the rule of law", with a vision of "A just society anchored on human rights and good governance" (MUHURI n.d.: 1).

From Christianity there is the example of the World Council of Churches (WCC) and its long history of human rights work on behalf of the worldwide ecumenical movement. Its work includes making statements condemning human rights violations in countries such as the Philippines, Israel, Iran, the Dominican Republic and Nigeria; delivering education programmes; and promoting practical advocacy work. Its advocacy work includes promoting the rights of stateless people, the rights and self-determination of Indigenous peoples across the globe, and gender justice and equality. In April 2022, through a conference organized jointly by the WCC, the Commission of the Churches on International Affairs, the United Evangelical Mission, and the Evangelical Church in Germany on the theme of "Christian Perspectives on Human Dignity and Human Rights", the message given to churches worldwide was to "rediscover the rich biblical narratives that affirm human dignity, justice and the rule of law" (WCC 2022: 1).

From Judaism is the example in the United States of the organization T'ruah: The Rabbinic Call for Human Rights, founded in 2002. The scope of their work is North America, Israel, and the occupied Palestinian territories. A three-pronged approach underpins their work:

> (i) Organize rabbis, cantors, and their communities to make an impact through specific human rights campaigns; (ii) train rabbinical and cantorial students and rabbis and cantors to be powerful human rights leaders; (iii) amplify the voices of rabbis and cantors on the pressing human rights concerns of our time.
>
> (T'ruah n.d.:1)

The foundation of their work is "to act on the Jewish imperative to respect and advance the human rights of all people. Grounded in Torah and our Jewish historical experience and guided by the Universal Declaration of Human Rights" (ibid.: 1).

Religious statements, declarations, and discourses

Since the second half of the twentieth century, several religious institutions and bodies have, as part of their engagement with human rights, issued statements and declarations primarily aimed at their religious communities but also aimed at contributing to the thought, policy, and practice of the non-religious areas of the public sphere. According to Witte and Green, these "have helped to mobilize human rights reflection and activism within these religious communities" (Witte and Green 2011: 12). Several examples can be given.

In the case of the Roman Catholic Church (RCC), *Rerum Novarum*, an encyclical of Pope Leo XIII, published in 1891, is identified as a significant development in the RCC's institutional recognition of the importance of human rights and the role of the Church in advocating these and articulating this through Catholic social teaching. In 1963, Pope John XXIII's Encyclical Letter *Pacem in Terris* identified human rights and duties of each person by virtue of *Imago Dei* (image of God). A more recent example is the public message delivered by Cardinal Peter Turkson on behalf of Pope Francis in 2018 at an International Conference on Human Rights in the Contemporary World at the Pontifical Gregorian University in Rome. In this message, Pope Francis identified three key issues that needed to be recognized: (1) the equal dignity of every human person, (2) human dignity cannot be ignored; (3) each person has the responsibility to help with protecting human rights (Merlo 2018: 1). Catholic Social Teaching, which has emerged through papal, conciliar, and episcopal documents, contains several key themes and concepts of which the following are especially pertinent to human rights: Life and Dignity of the Human Person, Rights, and Responsibilities, The Common Good, Option for the Poor and Vulnerable, Solidarity, Dignity, and Peace.

In the early 1970s, the Protestant churches also began issuing statements on human rights. These included the World Alliance of Reformed Churches (WARC), the Baptist World Congress (BWC), and the Lutheran World Federation (LWF). In 1970, the General Council of WARC recommended that a study be done on the theological basis of human rights and a theology of liberation. Various committees and groups of theologians were involved in this study, and in 1976 a final report from the study and a consensus statement representing WARC's position on human rights were approved. One year later, WARC sponsored a further study on the theological basis of human rights, this time on an ecumenical basis, involving Orthodox, Roman Catholic, Lutheran, and Reformed theologians concerned with the study of the theological basis of human rights, and this resulted in the publication of a further report and statement in 1980. In 1975, the BWC adopted a resolution on "Religious Liberty, Human Rights, World Peace and Public Morality". The opening of the section on human rights states: "We believe that God has made humankind in his own image and that he endows us with certain human rights which Christians are obligated to affirm, defend, and extend" (BWC 1975: 2). In 1977, at the Sixth Assembly of the LWF a statement was adopted on "Socio-political Functions and Responsibilities of Lutheran Churches"; the focus was the search for social and economic justice and the promotion of human dignity and rights. Advocacy of these issues was identified as "an essential, integral part of the mission of the church. It belongs inherently to the proclamation of the word" (LWF 2006: 9). Some 30 years later, a publication by the LWF titled *Faith and Human Rights*, reflecting on the 1977 LWF Assembly statement, concluded: "There is indeed much in Christian teaching and theology that enables churches to 'own' human rights as an essential part of their ministry" (ibid.).

A final example from Christianity is *The Kairos Document* (SAKD), an ecumenical document published in 1985 amidst the deteriorating political crisis in South Africa. The document has two subtitles: *Challenge to the Church* and *A Theological Comment on the Political Crisis in South Africa*. SAKD is a theological statement from a group of predominantly black South African theologians living and working in the townships of Johannesburg and Soweto. They aimed to challenge the misuse of Christian teachings both by the state and among Christian churches to justify apartheid which denied Black South Africans their rights because of government policies and laws of racial segregation and acts of violence committed by police and security forces. The authors of SAKD located their theological argument concerning the situation of oppression and racism in South Africa in the biblical accounts of the Israelites and their experience of oppression under the Egyptians, Babylonians, and Romans, and reference is made to episodes when ordinary and poor Israelites were oppressed under the rule of their own political and religious leaders

(Kairos Theologians 1985: 64–66). The critical challenge of SAKD to South African churches is that God takes sides with the oppressed:

> Throughout the Bible God appears as the liberator of the oppressed. He is not neutral. Oppression is a sin, and it cannot be compromised with, it must be done away with. God takes sides with the oppressed. As we read in Psalm 103:6, "God who does what is right, is always on the side of the oppressed.
>
> (ibid.: 25)

In Islam, there have been three Declarations. In 1981 came the Universal Islamic Declaration of Human Rights (UIDHR) from the Islamic Council based in London, affiliated with the Muslim World League in Paris. In the foreword of this document, it quotes the Quranic text, "This is a declaration for mankind, a guidance, and instruction to those who fear God" (Al Quran, Al-Imran 3:138), as grounds to argue: "Islam gave to mankind an ideal code of human rights fourteen centuries ago. These rights aim to confer honour and dignity on mankind and eliminate exploitation, oppression and injustice" (ICLMWL 1981: 1). The UIDHR identifies 23 aspects, including the right to life, freedom, equality, justice, and education; the right to protection against torture and abuse of power; and the right to freedom of religion, thought, speech, and free association. A second declaration, the Cairo Declaration on Human Rights in Islam, was issued in 1990 by the Organization of Islamic Cooperation, consisting of 45 states with Muslim-majority populations. The Cairo Declaration begins by stating that "All human beings form one family whose members are united by their subordination to Allah and descent from Adam", and therefore "All men are equal in terms of basic human dignity and basic obligations and responsibilities, without any discrimination on the basis of race, colour, language, belief, sex, religion, political affiliation, social status or other" (OIC 1990: 1). Article 24 states: "All the rights and freedoms stipulated in this Declaration are subject to the Islamic Shariah" (ibid.: 2). The third declaration is the Arab Charter on Human Rights passed at a meeting of the League of Arab States in May 2004. It has been accepted, at the time of writing, by ten Arab states. It affirms the universality and indivisibility of human rights and among the rights it recognizes are the right to education and healthcare, a fair trial, freedom from torture and ill-treatment, and the right to liberty. All three Islamic Declarations engage with human rights as presented in the 1948 UDHR and have much common agreement with UDHR. While the 1981 Islamic declaration "is more concerned with the freedom and rights of individuals", the 1990 declaration is considered predominantly aimed at protecting Islam in the context of classical Sharia and concerned with the security of the state (Masud 2012: 114). The third Declaration is less concerned with maintaining the dominance of Sharia, but it is considered by international legal experts and the UN to fall short of some of the standards of the UDHR; for example, on women's rights and the scope of the restrictions it allows on the exercise of freedom of thought, conscience, and religion (Rishmawi 2009: 2).

Debates and discussions have emerged among Buddhist thinkers in Asia, especially those within the Mahayana tradition. Their focus is on a human rights ethos to promote understanding of human rights and responsibilities across Buddhist communities, and it has been used to critique the reality of state and government practices in countries such as Myanmar, Sri Lanka, China's rule of Tibet, and Thailand. For example, in Thailand, two Buddhist scholars, Sulak Sivaraksa and Saneh Chamarik, applied Buddhist teachings during the 1980s and 1990s as a social critique of the social injustice and violation of human rights perpetrated by Thailand's government. The work of both scholars promotes the link between democratic development and human rights and the need for social justice advocacy based on the moral teachings of classical Buddhism. On a global scale is the work of Tenzin Gyatso, the fourteenth Dalai Lama, recognized for his advocacy of increased global equality, so that all people have equal rights to peace, freedom, equality, and dignity.

In Confucianism, several contemporary Chinese Confucian scholars have discussed its relationship with human rights. For example, Lee focuses on identifying if the concept of rights was present in Confucian virtue-based morality (Lee 1992). Wong argues that if human rights are about being a good person and participating in building a good and just society, this is contained within Confucian teaching regarding virtue and the community-based approach to creating and maintaining society and the relationships therein (Wong 1984, 2006). According to Chan, acting in a spirit of benevolence expressed through care or love for family, friends, and strangers is rooted in Confucian conceptual and ethical teachings which are intended "to protect and promote people's material needs and social relationships, things that are the concerns of social and economic rights" (Chan 2011: 99). Li argues "that our moral potentials can be the foundation of human dignity in Confucianism, which justifies human rights" (Li 2020: 31).

The examples provided here are positive examples of the commitment to human rights within various religions even though they have received mixed and sometimes hostile responses from members within the respective religious traditions and from governments and other secular bodies in various geopolitical locations across the globe.

Conclusion

At both macro and micro levels, many religions are engaging with the issues and reality of human rights and the secular international human rights body of declarations and laws. For some religions, there is a concern that the contemporary international human rights regime is a Western construct created through language and concepts that are not easily found or compatible with sacred texts and classical teachings. However, as shown in this chapter and in the four case studies that follow, religious actors can make a constructive contribution to human rights work. First, they have unique authority, legitimacy, and influence within their own religious traditions and have inside knowledge and understanding of the complexities of the faith and lived experience of their followers. Second, by drawing on sacred teachings, religious statements, and declarations, religious actors can articulate and formulate values and concepts conducive to human rights. Third, they can publicly critique and challenge the government, judiciary, or organizations, and other bodies within the public sphere as regards the appropriateness of their policies, approaches, and practices concerning human rights. Fourth, religious actors have the capacity to mobilize followers within their own religious communities and beyond to engage in practical ways that can advocate the essentiality of human rights.

References

Baptist World Congress (BWC). (1975). *Resolution on Religious Liberty, Human Rights, World Peace and Public Morality*. Accessed from https://baptistworld.org/resolution-on-religious-liberty-human-rights-world-peace-and-public-morality/ [Date accessed September 21, 2022].

Boyle, Kevin. (1995). "Stock-Taking on Human Rights: The World Conference on Human Rights, Vienna 1993", *Political Studies* XLIII: 79–95.

Chan, Joseph C.W. (2011). "Confucianism and Human Rights", in John Witte and Christian M. Green (eds.). *Religion and Human Rights: An Introduction*. Oxford: Oxford University Press, 87–102.

Glendon. Mary Ann. (2001). *A World Made New: Eleanor Roosevelt and the Universal Declaration of Human Rights*. New York: Random House.

Islamic Council London and Muslim World League (ICLMWL). (1981). *Universal Islamic Declaration of Human Rights*. London: Islamic Council.

Jaffrelot, Christopher. (2005). *Dr Ambedkar and Untouchability*. New Delhi: Permanent Black.

Kairos Theologians. (1985). *Kairos. The Moment of Truth: The Times Has Come. The Moment of Truth Has Arrived*. Geneva: World Council of Churches.

Kim, Kyungrae, and Cheonghwan Park. (2020). "Migrant Buddhist Communities and Korean "Multiculturalism" – A Brief Survey of the Issues Surrounding Support for South Korea's Immigrant Buddhist Communities", *Religions* 11 (12): 1–11. Accessed from Iswww.mdpi.com/2077-1444/11/12/628/htm [Date accessed September 19, 2022].

Lee, Seung-hwan. (1992). "Was There a Concept of Rights in Confucian Virtue-Based Morality?", *Journal of Chinese Philosophy* 19: 241–261.

Li, Yong. (2020). "Confucianism and the Foundation of Human Rights", in Zhibin Xie, Pauline Kollontai, and Sebastian Kim (eds.). *Human Dignity, Human Rights and Social Justice: A Chinese Interdisciplinary Dialogue with Global Perspective*. Singapore: Springer, 19–32.

Lutheran World Federation (LWF). (2006). *Faith and Human Rights Voices from the Lutheran Communion*. Minnesota, MN: Lutheran University Press Minneapolis.

Masud, Muhammad Khalid. (2012). "Clearing Ground: Shari'a and the Modern State", in Emon M. Anver, Marc S. Ellis, and Benjamin Glahn (eds.). *Islamic Law and International Human Rights Law*. Oxford: Oxford University Press, 104–114.

Merlo, Francesco. (2018). "Pope: Human Rights First, Even if it Means Going Against the Tide", *Vatican News*, December 10, 2018. Accessed from www.vaticannews.va/en/pope/news/2018-12/pope-francis-message-human-rights-day-international-conference.html [Date accessed September 27, 2021].

Muslims for Human Rights (MUHURI). (n.d.). *About Us*. Accessed from https://muhuri.org/about-us/ [Date accessed January 10, 2022].

Organization of Islamic Cooperation (OIC). (1990). *The Cairo Declaration on Human Rights in Islam*. Accessed from www.oic-oci.org/upload/pages/conventions/en/CDHRI_2021_ENG.pdf [Date accessed October 10, 2021].

Rishmawi, Mervat. (2009). "The Arab Charter on Human Rights", Briefing Paper. Carnegie Endowment for International Peace. Accessed from https://carnegieendowment.org/sada/23951 [Date accessed September 21, 2022].

Sadhana. (n.d.). *Mission, Vision and Values*. Accessed from www.sadhana.org/mission-vision-values [Date accessed September 21, 2022].

T'ruah. (n.d.). *About Us*. Accessed from https://truah.org/about/ [Date accessed December 21, 2021].

United Nations Department of Public Information (UNDPI). (1949). *Yearbook of the United Nations 1947–1948*. New York: UN Department of Public Information.

United Nations General Assembly (UNGA). (1948). *United Nations Declaration of Human Rights*. Accessed from www.un.org/en/about-us/universal-declaration-of-human-rights [Date accessed December 5, 2021].

United Nations Human Rights Office of the High Commissioner (UNHROHC). (1993). *Vienna Declaration and Programme of Action*. Accessed from www.ohchr.org/en/instruments-mechanisms/instruments/vienna-declaration-and-programme-action [Date accessed September 21, 2022].

Witte, John, and M. Christian Green. (2011). "Introduction", in John Witte and M. Christian Green (eds.). *Religion and Human Rights: An Introduction*. Oxford: Oxford University Press, 3–24.

Wong, David B. (2006). *Natural Moralities: A Defense of Pluralistic Relativism*. New York: Oxford.

Wong, David B. (1984). *Moral Relativity*. Berkeley, CA: University of California Press.

World Council of Churches (WCC). (2022). *Conference Calls on Churches to Listen, Speak the Truth and Advocate for Human Rights*. April 13, 2022. Accessed from www.oikoumene.org/news/conference-calls-on-churches-to-listen-speak-the-truth-and-advocate-for-human-rights [Date accessed September 21, 2022].

Zucchino, David, and Yaqoob Akbary. (2022). "Threatened and Beaten, Afghan Women Defy Taliban with Protests", *The New York Times*, January 24, 2022. Accessed from www.nytimes.com/2022/01/24/world/asia/afghan-women-taliban-protests.html [Date accessed January 28, 2022].

4.2

HINDU PERSPECTIVE

Women and Democratic Ideals in Hinduism: A Case Study of Women's Entrance to Sabarimala Temple

Hari Priya Pathak

Introduction

Cultural practices, beliefs, attitudes, and views in Hinduism (*Sanatan Dharma*), as a way of life, are governed and structured by the earliest scriptures like the *Vedas*, the *Upanishads*, the *Smritis*, and *Puranas*. The Democratic ideals seen in the actions of some contemporary women have their roots in the Vedic period (1500 to 600 BCE). This chapter discusses democratic ideals in Hinduism regarding women, beginning from the Vedic to the present times, and how history, colonialism, post-colonialism, scientific and technological developments, and the spread of human rights influenced these. It then discusses the case of women's entry to the Sabarimala Temple (2018) which raised important issues of gender equality, fundamental rights, religious practices, and women's rights.

Women in Hinduism – from Vedic to Mughal periods

The Vedic period (1500 to 600 BCE) is considered a golden period for women in Hinduism. *Upanayan Sanskaar*, a ceremony to begin formal education for both girls and boys, provided freedom for women to take up higher studies (philosophy and logic) with the aim of becoming *Brahmavadinis* and *Upadhayayanis* (women gurus) like Romsha, Lopamudra, Aditi, and Shikhandini. Women participated in religious rituals, composing several hymns in the *Rig Veda*, and there was an absence of Sati and dowry. The *Vedas* show a deep reverence for the feminine. The *Devi Sukta* hymn, in the tenth chapter of the *Rig Veda*, affirms the feminine principle behind all creation.

The later Vedic period (800 to 500 BCE), known for the *Upanishads*, is replete with matters of spirituality relating, for example, to Brahman, Atman, karma, and salvation, where women like *Gargi*, *Maitreyi*, *Usati*, and *Satyakama* composed hymns

DOI: 10.4324/9781003344537-13

and participated in spiritual debates. *Brihadaranynaka Upanishad* contains many hymns regarding the birth of a son and has one for the birth of a learned daughter:

> And if a man wishes that a learned daughter should be born to him, and that she should live to her full age, then, after having prepared boiled rice with sesamum and butter, they should both eat, being fit to have offspring.
>
> (Muller 1965: 6.4.17)

In the period of the *Dharmasastras* (legal texts) from 400 to 100 BCE, scriptures like *Smritis*, including the *Puranas*, the *Ramayana*, and the *Mahabharata*, showed the "prominence of Brahmins in rituals, stratification of society in castes and prohibition of mobility across the caste boundaries, to be maintained strictly by regulating marriages and eating arrangements" (Murray 1994: 206–207), and led to a deterioration of women's social condition. *Smritis*, especially *Manusmriti*, has injunctions on morality and social codes pertaining to women with statements shifting from derogation to glorification. For example: "She who, controlling her thoughts, speech, and acts, violates not her duty towards her lord, dwells with him (after death) in heaven, and in this world is called by the virtuous a faithful wife, Sadhvi" (Buhler 1886: IX, 29), and "Where women are honoured, there the gods are pleased; but where they are not honoured, no sacred rite yields reward" (Buhler 1886: III, 56). However, the *Puranas*, marking the end of the Vedic period, show a glorification of the sacred feminine in texts like *Devi Mahatmya*, *Markendeya Maha-Purana*, and *Devi-Bhagwat Purana*.

The changing sociocultural scene (400 to 100 BCE), with the rise of Brahmin-dominated patriarchal society, rituals, superstitions, and beliefs, led to a degradation in the position of women. Prohibition of widow remarriage and *Upanayana Sanskar*, now considered equivalent to marriage for women, led to early marriages. *Stridhan* (later became dowry) also emerged by the end of the Vedic period. With all these elements present, the Islamic invasions from the seventh century CE onwards acted as the final nail in the coffin, "Due to fear of abduction and molestation by Muslim invaders; child marriages, purdah system, restriction on the free movement of women and their education became an inherent part of medieval Hindu society" (Rawat and Kumar 2015: 86). Evil practices like *Sati* and *Jauhar* became common. However, there were women warriors and administrators like Queen Durgawati, Shivaji's mother Jijabai, and Ahilya Bai Holkar, and the Bhakti movement with women like Meera Bai, Akkamahadevi, Habbakhatun, and Chandravati who tried during this period to "restore women's status by providing them equal footing with men, thus questioning their subservient status and openly advocating equality among men and women" (Rawat and Kumar 2015: 86).

Women before independence

During British rule (1858–1947), reformers like Ram Mohan Roy, Ishwar Chandra Vidyasagar, Dayanand Saraswati, and Jyotiba Phule, fought for women's education, opposed *sati* and child marriage, advocated widow remarriage and abolition of *purdah* (seclusion and isolation of women from public observations through clothing like the veil and high-walled enclosure, screens, curtains). Christian missionaries passed several laws against these social evils and spread education among women. Also, "The Gandhian concept of 'Shakti in Modern India' envisaged induction of women into the struggle for liberation. [. . .] He [Gandhi] initiated the process of liberation of Indian women and ratified women's power" (Misra 2006: 870). Women like Sarojini Naidu, Lakshmi Menon, and Sushila Nayyar rose to prominence, and others participated wholeheartedly in this process. Several women's regional organizations like Bharat Stri Mandal (1910), Sharda Sadan, Bhagini Samaj (1916), the Maternity and Child Welfare League (1914), and national organizations like the Women's India Association (1917), The National Council of Women (1920) and All India Women's Conference (1926) were formed.

Post-independence and women

Beginning with the Committee on the Status of Women (1974), *stri shakti* (women's power) established itself as a great force in changing the status and rights of women in the private and public spheres. In the early 1970s, many women participated in the anti-price rise movement forming the Anti-Price Rise Women's Committee, the *Stree Mukti Sangathan* and the Progressive Organization of Women. With the UN's declaration of 1975–1985 as a women's decade, and the 1975–1977 state of emergency in India, declared by President Indira Gandhi's government for prevailing "internal and external disturbances", many women's groups, as depicted in seminar articles, media and journals like *Manushi* and publications like *Kali*, protested the atrocities and human rights violations that occurred during the emergency period.

Examples of activist movements are the Chipko Movement (1970s), when women from the hills rose against the authorities preventing the felling of the trees by embracing them, and the Anti-Arrack movement (1990s) when nearly 40,000 women united against the Arrack (local liquor) sale causing alcoholism among men leading to domestic violence. Several women's organizations and non-governmental organizations (NGOs) actively worked against rape, dowry murders, child marriages, and domestic violence through rallies and campaigns forcing the government to amend the laws. Beginning with the Mathura Rape Case in 1972 and the Nirbhaya Case in 2012, Indian women have been transformed from helpless creatures to politically conscious beings.

Hindu goddesses as symbol of *stri shakti*

Hinduism is the only religion in the world having a tradition of goddess worship where her presence is "not only the existence and worship of the goddess, but also her representations in 'feminist' ways – as complementary 'female principle', as an autonomous female agent or as a powerful cosmic force", writes Rajeswari Sundar

Rajan (1998: 2). The presence of goddesses in feminine form empowers women by imparting them "a certain sense of dignity, self-worth, personal assertiveness and simple visibility" (Gross 1978: 274).

These goddesses are symbols of revolt, strength, hope, and transformation for women. Lina Gupta asks: "How can contemporary women identify themselves with a mythical character? I think there is an interaction between contemporary woman's psyche and the mythic behavior patterns that inform and are played out in a woman's life" (Gupta 1991: 36). Jessica Raja-Brown notes, in "Kali: Goddess and Revolutionary", how Kali's image was feared and misrepresented as a demonic figure by the British and Christian missionaries and how the Bengal independence movement exploited the British fear of Kali (Raja-Brown 2021: 4–5).

The images of goddesses are frequently used for campaigning in India against rape and domestic violence. "Abused Goddess" was one such campaign against domestic violence started in 2010 by an NGO "Save the Children India". The second was a digital comic book, "Priya's Shakti" released in 2014, made accessible with the help of the NGO "Apne Aap Worldwide". It depicts the story of a rape survivor who realizes her own *shakti* after encountering the Goddess Parvati. Moreover, religious myths and symbols related to the goddess figures of Sita, Draupadi, and others are being continuously renegotiated, reinterpreted, and revised to create contextual meaning with the changing times by contemporary writers like Chitra Banerjee Divakaruni and Amish Tripathi.

Sabarimala temple entrance (2018): a case study

Sabarimala Temple is a temple worshipping Lord Ayyappa in Kerala, India, known for its pilgrimage, lasting 41 days, made exclusively by men after fulfilling *vratham* (fasting) and other rituals. Women were traditionally prohibited to undertake such a journey to worship Lord Ayyappa. This prohibition was made legal for women of reproductive age (between 10 and 50) by the Kerala High Court in 1991. The court stated that such a restriction, introduced by the Devaswom Board of the temple, was in accordance with customs and it did not violate Articles 15, 25, and 26 of the Indian Constitution or the provisions of the 1965 Hindu Place of Public Worship (Authorisation of Entry) Act, which contains no restriction of any class or social sections but only restriction of women of a particular age group but not women as a class. (Srivastava 2018).

Origin of the Sabarimala entrance case

In 2006, six women from the Indian Young Lawyers Association petitioned (Public Interest Litigation [PIL]) India's Supreme Court to lift the 1991 ban against women of reproductive age entering Sabarimala, arguing that the practice was in violation of their constitutional rights and questioning the validity of provisions in the 1965 Kerala Hindu Places of Public Worship Rules Act which supported it. In 2007, the Government of Kerala filed an affidavit supporting the PIL, which was considered by the Supreme Court in 2008, but no judgement was passed. A change of government in Kerala occurred in 2011 and the new government withdrew its support for the previous government's affidavit. In 2016, the Supreme Court established a three-judge bench to consider a petition submitted by the NGO "Right to Bleed", concerning discrimination against women based on the biological process of menstruation. Also, in 2016, a new government in Kerala was elected that supported women's entry to Sabarimala. In 2017, the three-judge bench produced significant questions regarding the merits of the case, and it was transferred to a five-judge Constitution bench. The hearing took place, and the final verdict was given in 2018.

Arguments in favour of women's entry to the temple

The lawyers petitioning for the entry of women to Sabarimala based their arguments against the impugned rules of the Devaswom Board mainly on the violation of Articles 14, 15, 21, 17, and 25, concerning justice, liberty, equality, fraternity, and dignity of an individual as stated in the Constitution's Preamble. They argued the practice of banning women was manifestly arbitrary and based on physiological factors discriminating on the bases of "sex" alone which promoted stereotypes of a particular gender and stigmas that presented women as polluters, a form of untouchability akin to lepers and beggars, producing a negative psychological impact on women. It was a form of untouchability. They said that the devotees of Lord Ayyappa did not constitute a religious denomination, and the prohibition of women entering Sabarimala was not an essential practice because it did not constitute the core foundation of Hinduism.

Based on several prior cases, they stated that various Hindu philosophical concepts and principles evolved by different thinkers and philosophers revered and accepted the *Vedas* as the sole foundation of Hindu philosophy, and Vedic philosophy is progressive in nature. In Hindu philosophy, argued the lawyers, "there is no scope for excommunicating any notion or principle as heretical and rejecting it as such", and the Hindu religion is not tied to any definite set of philosophical concepts (Jaising 2016: 43). Several saints and religious reformers from time to time cleansed Hinduism of corruption and practices based on blind beliefs and superstitions. The Devaswom Board, they said, had failed in its responsibilities and was dependent on certain superstitions in its work. They argued that India is a modern democracy and therefore it was the responsibility of the court to create an egalitarian society based on the Indian Constitution, and that India is a signatory to international norms and conventions such as the *Convention of the Elimination of all Forms of Discrimination Against Women*, which mandates to overcome, dismantle and refrain from promoting gender stereotypes.

Arguments against the entry of women

Those opposed to lifting the prohibition rested their arguments mainly on the 1991 Kerala High Court judgement restricting women's entry to Sabarimala. They stated that the petitioners represented a handful of women who disregarded traditions and were "keen to avoid the violation of its sacrosanct traditions by others under the façade of gender equality" (Deepak 2018: 5). They emphatically said that the restriction on the entry of women was not associated with menstruation but with the celibate nature (*Naisthik Bramchari*) of the deity who, it is believed, would be deviated in the presence of young women offering prayers. They argued that the temple followed the rituals and practices based on *Agama Sastras* and the final decision on these matters rested upon the *thantris* (priests). If the *thantris* were unable to decide, they would use *Devaprasnam* (questions to the Deity). They emphasized that the Devaswom Board must implement the wishes of the Deity. Based on the 1991 Kerala High Court's judgement, the opposition reiterated the argument that devotees of Lord Ayyappa constituted a denomination and had rights under Articles 25 and 26 to have their own rules and regulations in religious matters. They noted that there are many Hindu temples in India worshipping the act of menstruation, and some temples that restricted men's entry. They stressed that the Deity had a legal personage under Indian law: He has rights as a person under Articles 25(1), 26, and 21, therefore the Deity in His abode must have the right to privacy, and the state was bound to protect this right of the Deity as an individual (ibid.: 5–9).

Supreme Court verdict

On September 28, 2018, the Supreme Court of India ruled that women of all age groups could enter Sabarimala temple:

> While the Constitution recognizes religious beliefs and faiths, its purpose is to ensure a wider acceptance of human dignity and liberty as the ultimate founding faith of the fundamental text of our governance. Where a conflict arises, the quest for human dignity, liberty and equality must prevail.
>
> (Chandrachud 2018: 15)

The court dismissed the practice of women's prohibition to enter the temple stating that it was not an essential religious practice and would not alter the fundamental nature of the religion. The practice was said to stereotype women as being weak and lesser human beings. The court dismissed the assumption of imposing the burden of a man's celibacy on a woman and maintained that any practice to be protected by law should not be based on superstitions, ignorance, and misunderstanding of the true teachings of Hindu philosophy. In the final judgement, Judge Chandrachud cited Tilak's definition of Hinduism:

> Acceptance of the Vedas with reverence; recognition of the fact that the means or ways to salvation are diverse and realization of the truth that the number of gods to be worshipped is large, that indeed is the distinguishing feature of Hindu religion.
>
> (Ibid.: 59)

The court declared that the devotees of Lord Ayyappa do not satisfy the judicially enunciated requirements to constitute a religious denomination under Article 26 of the Constitution. The court also stated that the social exclusion of women, based on menstrual status, is a form of untouchability and an anathema to constitutional values, and notions of "purity and pollution", which stigmatize women by affecting their right to freedom and education, thus, limiting their public space (ibid.: 115).

Resistance, protests, and strikes against the verdict

Immediate resistance occurred when Sabarimala reopened in October 2018 for pilgrims. Many women journalists were assaulted by the protestors and driven away. Several protests and strikes were organized in Kerala by various political groups. Both Congress and the Bhartiya Janta Party launched protests demanding the government file a review petition against the verdict. Over 3,000 people were arrested and a further 500 people were registered for possible arrest.

In November 2018, Section 144 of the Indian Penal Code, denying assembly of people in possible danger, was declared at places close to the temple for the 41-day-long pilgrim season. On December 26, across Kerala, thousands of Ayyappa devotees, mainly women, took part in "Ayyappa Jyothi", an event organized by Hindutva organizations protesting against the Supreme Court verdict. This protest was countered by around 3 to 5 million women forming a human chain called *Vanitha Mathil*, as part of another event organized by the Kerala state government in support of the verdict.

Successful entry of women to Sabarimala

The first women to enter the Sabarimala Temple (not via the 18 sacred steps but via the staff gate) with a police escort on January 2, 2019 were Bindu Ammini (aged 40) and Kanakadurga (aged 39); both stayed at secret locations before reaching the temple. Protests occurred and the temple was closed briefly for purification. Once reopened many more women of menstrual age were said to "dodge" protestors and successfully entered Sabarimala during this pilgrimage season. A woman Dalit leader (aged 38) entered the temple and posted videos and photos to a Facebook group called "*Navodhana Keralam Sabarimalayilekku*" ('Renaissance Kerala to Sabarimala').

Aftermath

On November 14, 2019, the Supreme Court referred the Sabarimala case to a bench of seven judges because several review petitions were submitted. The judges were asked to investigate various religious issues, including the right of all women to enter the Sabarimala temple and mosques, Parsi Fire temples, and the practice of female genital mutilation in the Dawoodi Bohra community. As of October 2022, no further decision has been made concerning the Sabarimala case. Various women's empowerment groups like *Saheli* and *Bharatiya Samajik Jagritik Sanghatan*, along with other activists, have expressed discontent with how the Supreme Court has given the impression that verdicts are influenced by what pleases or displeases those in power. Others like Rahul Easwar, petitioner and social activist, consider the review to be a positive step.

Conclusion

The 2018 Supreme Court decision upheld women's human rights but the Sabarimala case was transferred to a larger judicial bench for review after a year because of the protests and review petitions, representing the ongoing influence of political parties and public votes. In this decision, the court rightly emphasized that practices that discriminate based on religion must be checked for their essentiality and should not be based on superstitions as "scriptures and customs merge with bewildering complexity into superstition and dogma" (ibid.: 22). The *Vedas* and the Hindu religion were referred to in the court's verdict, alongside an emphasis on the human dignity and rights of individuals as stated in the Constitution. This 2018 judgement paves hope for womenfolk in India. Many women hope that the current seven-judge bench will do further justice to women's human rights that have been pending for a long time.

References

Buhler, G. (1886). *The Laws of Manu*. Oxford: Clarendon Press.

Chandrachud, Justice. (2018). "In the Supreme Court of India Civil Original Jurisdiction", Writ Petition (Civil) No. 373 of 2006. Judgement. Accessed from file:///C:/Users/Hi/Downloads/18956_2006_Judgement_28-Sep-2018–172–336%20JUSTICE%20CHANDRACHUD.pdf [Date accessed October 19, 2022].

Deepak, Sai. (2018). "In the Supreme Court of India Civil Original Jurisdiction", I.A. No. 30 of 2016. Writ Petition (Civil) No. 373 of 2006. Accessed from file:///C:/Users/Hi/Downloads/People_For_Dharma%20SAI%20DEEPAK.pdf [Date accessed October 19, 2022].

Gross, Rita M. (1978). "Female Deities as a Resource for the Contemporary Rediscovery of the Goddess", *Journal of the American Academy of Religion* 46 (3): 269–291.

Gupta, Lina. (1991). "Kali, the Savior", in Paula M. Cooey, William R. Eakin, and Jay B. McDaniel (eds.). *After Patriarchy: Feminist Transformations of World Religions*. New York: Orbis Books, 15–38.

Jaising, Indira. (2016). "In the Supreme Court of India Civil Original Jurisdiction", I.A. No. 10 of 2016. Writ Petition (Civil) No. 373 of 2006. Accessed from file:///C:/Users/Hi/Downloads/Sabarimala_Indira_Jaising_Written_Submissions.doc__1_.pdf [Date accessed October 19, 2022].

Misra, Jugal Kishore. (2006). "Empowerment of Women in India", *The Indian Journal of Political Science* 67 (4): 867–878.

Muller, Max. (1965). *The Upanishads*. Translated by Max Muller. Delhi: Motilal Banarasidass Publishers.

Murray, Milner Jr. (1994). *Status and Sacredness: A General Theory of Status Relations and an Analysis of Indian Culture*. Oxford: Oxford University Press.

Raja-Brown, Jessica. (2021). "Kali: Goddess and Revolutionary", *Varsity*, January 15, 2021.

Rajan, Rajeswari Sundar. (1998). "Is the Hindu Goddess a Feminist?", *Economic and Political Weekly* 33 (44): 34–38.

Rawat, Sugandha, and Pradeep Kumar. (2015). "Hindu Women in the Mirror of Time: At Once a Goddess and Slave?", *Journal of Indian Research* 3 (3): 82–91.

Srivastava, Saumya. (2018). "Sabrimala Temple Entry Ban for Women: What Are the Major Questions before the Constitution Bench?", *The Leaflet*, July 17, 2018.

4.3

JEWISH PERSPECTIVE

Challenging Jewish Religious Exclusionist Praxis

Pauline Kollontai

Introduction

The contemporary human rights system can be seen as representing a system of values and concepts embedded in key beliefs that make up the essence of Jewish sacred writings and rabbinic teachings. Therefore, by relooking at this, a case can be made that Judaism can and does have a role in promoting and supporting human rights. One way this is manifesting is through the values, principles, and work of the Jewish-founded religious-based organization *Tag Meir* (TM) (Light Tagging) to help remove racism and violence in Israeli society. This organization focuses on challenging those religious Jews who ignore and violate key religious beliefs and also on challenging and providing a stark reminder to the Israeli state, as a Jewish and democratic entity, that Torah-based teachings of justice, dignity, and peace are enshrined in the 1948 Declaration of the Founding of the State of Israel. These teachings form an important part of the Israeli state's commitment that complete equality of social, political, and religious rights to all its inhabitants, irrespective of religion, race, or sex, will be ensured. Consideration of TM's work is important to demonstrate the potential of Jews to reclaim and assert their prophetic heritage and teachings which combine to safeguard the existence and rights of all people.

"Judaism contains the concept of human rights"

Some scholars see the modern system of human rights as "a modern juridical notion representing a system of values and concepts which can be found among the beliefs which constitute the very core of Jewish sacred scripture and the tradition of ideas and practices which flows from it" (Polish 1982: 40). Although there is no exact word in classical Hebrew to the modern term "rights", there are equivalents

DOI: 10.4324/9781003344537-14

to the term "duty", as in "commandments" (*mitzvot*) and "obligations" (*hovot*). Novak argues: "For the very concept of duty cannot stand on its own without the correlative concept of rights. After all, a duty is something one owes to someone else" (Novak 1996: 69). Brichto states: "Although there is the absence of an explicit vocabulary of human rights in the Bible, what is needed is the interpretation of biblical thought that requires the translation of concepts rather than of words" (Brichto 1979: 215–216).

So, what are the key concepts and values found in the Torah that can support the existence and practice of human rights? Duties to others as set out in biblical and classical Judaism are underpinned by the belief in *Tzelem Elohim* (human beings are created in the image of God), and therefore respect for the divine image in each person is an essential aspect of duty and responsibility. The Torah teachings of compassion for others are expressed through *Gemilut Hasadim* (performing acts of loving-kindness), doing justice, and practising concern for dignity and sanctity of life. The Torah and the Talmud reference God as the Compassionate One (*Rahamanan*). On the one hand, the practice of God's compassion is rooted explicitly in the covenantal relationship between God and the Israelites. On the other, it is part of *Lihidamot* or emulating God in the world through compassionate acts as an essential part of human conduct as stated in Midrash on the book of Deuteronomy, "Just as God is called compassionate and gracious, so you must be compassionate and gracious" (MDSif. Dev. 11: 49). As recorded in the Babylonian Talmud, the Rabbis consider compassion one of the three distinguishing marks of being a Jew (BTYeb 1938: 79a). Maimonides argued that those who were arrogant, cruel, and unloving, should be suspected of not being Jews (Maimonides 1190). Also, the Jewish teachings of *Va'ahavtem et ha-Ger* (love of stranger) and *Ve'ahabhath le-re'akha* (love of neighbour) can be seen as central to the concept and practice of human rights for all human beings. Examples are found in Leviticus 19: 33–34: "When a stranger resides with you in your land, you shall not wrong him. The stranger who resides with you shall be to as one of your citizens; you shall love him as yourself"; further teachings on this issue are found in Leviticus 23:22, 24:22, and Exodus 22:21. The importance of not oppressing the stranger appears in Exodus 23: 9, practising justice towards the stranger is specified in Deuteronomy 24:18, and unjust treatment is identified as a serious violation of God's commands (Deut. 27:19). Other teachings provide a code of behaviour between neighbours. Examples are found in the Ten Commandments (Exodus 20: 1–17). In Leviticus, the importance of treating a neighbour fairly and not perverting justice is stated (Lev. 19:15). The exploitation of neighbour is warned against in Jeremiah because it repudiates justice and righteousness (Jer. 22:13). Some Jewish scholars argue that the neighbour teachings refer only to Jews. Still, others such as Rabbi Ben Azzai (2 CE), the Rabbi and Kabbalist; Pinchas Elijah Hurwitz (1765–1821); Rabbi Chaim Hirschensohn, an Orthodox Zionist thinker (1857–1935); and the twenty-first-century Conservative Rabbi Reuven Hammer (1933–2019) believe the concept of neighbour to be a universal one, applicable to Jews and non-Jews. The major challenge for Jewish scholars, rabbis, and their communities throughout the centuries is interpreting religious teachings from a specific geopolitical, historical, and cultural context into their current time and reality.

Human rights in Israeli secular law

Israel does not have a constitution. Instead, it has a system of Basic Laws. It was not until the 1980s that work began developing two new Basic Laws that addressed human rights. In 1992, Knesset passed *The Basic Law on Human Dignity and Liberty* (BLHDL) and *The Basic Law on Freedom and Occupation*. The BLHDL was particularly important as its central aim is "to protect human dignity and liberty of all Israel's citizens, to establish in Basic Law the values of the State of Israel as a Jewish and democratic state" (Knesset BLHDL 1992: Sec. 1). In addition to these two Basic Laws, the Statute 5758, *Thou Shalt Not Stand Idly by the Blood of Thy Neighbour*, regarding another person's safety and possible death was passed in 1998. In the explanatory notes accompanying this statute, the purpose "is to anchor in Israeli legislation the moral and social value whose source is in the Torah (Lev. 19:16), according to which an obligation is imposed upon a person to save the life of another person" (Maoz 2004: 701). Despite these recent laws, the promotion and protection of the rights of Israel's non-Jewish citizens are inconsistent and often seriously lacking. This is partly the product of constructing a Jewish and democratic state in which the dominant Jewish establishment espouses a religious nationalism in which the Jewish teachings mentioned earlier have little meaning or importance concerning Israel's non-Jewish citizens. However, not all of Israel's Jewish citizens who identify in some way as religious adopt this stance, as illustrated in the next section through the example of the Jewish faith-based organization TM.

TM: practising Jewish teachings against violence and racism

Several organizations in Israel engage in ways to promote, advocate, and engage in a range of aspects of human rights work. Some of these are faith-based, and others are not. Jewish faith-based organizations include the *Israel Religious Action Centre*, founded in 1984, involving various work to create a pluralistic and egalitarian Israel in the ongoing pursuit of a just society. The *Inter-religious Coordinating Council* in Israel aims to bring together the teachings, values, and members of Judaism, Christianity, and Islam to promote and demonstrate religion's role in Israel as a source of promoting a peaceful and just coexistence between Jews and non-Jews. The organization *Rabbis for Human Rights* (RHR), founded in 1988 as a response to the violation of human rights taking place in the Occupied Territories, engages in advocacy and legal support, lobbying government educational activities, public events, and practical support to Palestinians living in the Occupied Territories. RHR identifies its work as rooted in the Jewish tradition, which at its heart "is the call to advance the dignity and protect the rights of all individuals" (RHR 2020: 1). *B'Tselem* (BTS) was founded in 1989 and works to end Israel's occupation of the territories it has taken since 1948. The name *B'Tselem* means "in the image of" and references Genesis 1:27: "And God created humankind in His image. In the image of God did He create them". BTS Board members say: "The name [*B'Tselem*] expresses the Jewish and universal moral edict to respect and uphold the human rights of all people", and this is the central aim of BTS (BTS 2020: 1). The work of BTS documents Israeli violations of Palestinians' human rights in the West Bank, East Jerusalem, and the Gaza Strip and publishes statistics, testimonies, and eyewitness accounts through reports and video footage, press releases, and public campaigns.

The most recent example is the organization TM, founded in 2011 by Dr Gadi Gvaryahu, a politically moderate Orthodox Israeli Jew, in response to the extreme actions of those settlers as discussed in the previous case study. TM is an umbrella organization of religious and secular groups concerned with challenging and over-coming the actions of any Israeli Jews who promote and engage in acts of violence and racism. Jewish religious extremists carry out violent attacks against the Israeli Arab community (Muslim and Christian) and the Reform and Conservative Jew-ish communities. TM has gained support from individuals and groups across the Reform, Conservative, Orthodox, and Ultra-Orthodox Jewish communities. TM's work is described as "part of a campaign to support democratic values and the very traditional Jewish values of loving our neighbours and justice for all" (TM n.d.: 1). On the one hand, it does this by challenging Jewish religious extremists for their actions and the Jewish Orthodox religious establishment for promoting an exclusionist theology regarding the land of Israel. On the other, TM identify and challenge all levels of government and state which promote, allow, and sometimes acquiesce with the speech and acts of prejudice, mistrust, and hatred of non-Jews. TM's overall message is that living and coexisting peacefully with non-Jews and upholding rights and justice for all is an essential part of a democracy and a cor-nerstone of the ethical demands of the Jewish tradition towards the neighbour and stranger. It does this through a range of work and activities.

In showing solidarity with the victims of Jewish religious extremist attacks, TM organizes help to clear up the aftermath of vandalism and destruction of homes, religious buildings, and other properties and often offers financial support. Inher-ent in these acts of solidarity is a critical challenge to the Jewish religious extrem-ists. TM does not shy away from publicly criticizing such extremists, as seen in May 2022 when Jewish settlers pepper-sprayed a Palestinian man and woman and their two-month-old baby as they waited at an Israeli military checkpoint near the West Bank village of Burqa. The baby required medical treatment. In response, TM released a short statement on social media. It referred to the perpetrators as "Jewish terrorists" and criticized the Israeli Defence Force and the government by stating: "The Jewish terrorists continue to operate without anyone stopping them". The statement ended with the words, "shame and disgrace" directed at both the perpetrators and the bystanders (TM 2022a: 1).

TM's work promotes further public awareness of such violence and racism, aiming to overcome the barriers of prejudice and mistrust between the various communities through the interfaith celebration of festivals, university and college campus outreach programmes, conferences, dialogue meetings, exhibitions, and public meetings and vigils. This organization's annual Flower Parade for Peace, through the Old City in Jerusalem, held on Jerusalem Day, is an act of solidarity with the Muslim residents and shop owners that aims to counteract the message of hatred and violence by right-wing religious Jews who march through the Muslim Quarter of the Old City waving the Israeli flag and chanting racist slogans such as: "Muhammad is dead" and "Vengeance avenges one of the two eyes of Palestine – their name will be erased" (TM 2019: 1). Usually, Muslim residents stay in their homes, and shop owners close their businesses until the march of the right-wing religious Jews has passed through. The TM Flower Parade for Peace involves its members distributing flowers to Muslims, conversing with them, and buying from their shops. At the 2022 Parade, a TM flyer was also distributed which said:

> Dear Neighbours, residents of the Old City. We have come today to reach out to you on this complicated day – to distribute flowers and purchase from your stores. We are sorry that the day is causing harm to your business and livelihood – "You shall love truth and peace".
>
> (TM 2022b: 1)

In the political and legal spheres, TM engages in lobbying and meeting with politicians and decision-makers on the political and legal fronts to ask them to act to end inflammatory incitement and rhetoric. TM regularly petitions the High Court of Justice through its legal team to ensure law enforcement is taken against Jewish religious extremists who incite and perpetuate violent hate and race crimes (TM 2017). In a media interview, Gadi Gvaryahu, founder and executive director of TM, referred to the acts of Jewish religious extremists as "Acts of terror perpetrated by Jews. Jewish terrorism, in short" (Shani 2017: 1). Ghalyah, who is an "Insider", a religiously observant Jew from a family that has lived for over eight generations in Israel, said:

> I am not willing to accept these people who have gone out in the dark of night, wearing kippot, and who in the name of Judaism decided to enter a mosque or assassinate a prime minister. They are turning Judaism, of which I am an integral part, into something different and frightening. Judaism is not a murderous religion.
>
> (Shani 2017: 2)

TM also challenges the actions and policies of state departments and governments concerning policies and actions that are considered to interfere with and deny human rights. An example is their response to Prime Minister (PM) Netanyahu's campaign announced in January 2018 to expel asylum seekers who arrived in the early twenty-first century from Sudan and Eritrea of Christian and Muslim backgrounds. The numbers of Eritreans residing in Israel in early 2018 were 26,081, and Sudanese totalled 7,481 (IPIBA 2018: 4). In the previous year the Israeli state publicly designated them as "economic migrants" whom it said the state could not and should not have to care about. These Sudanese and Eritreans had fled politically repressive regimes with high levels of human rights violations. Recognizing that these refugees could not be deported back to their country of origin, the Israeli state was brokering deals with third countries in Africa, such as Congo, Rwanda, and Uganda, to deport them too. In its letter, TM reminded PM Netanyahu of two specific Jewish teachings. First, "The stranger who lives among you will be like yourselves, and you will love him as yourself, for you were strangers in the land of Egypt" (Lev. 19:34) and, second, asking that the Israeli state

> Adopt the Jewish ethical principle [found in the Book of Deuteronomy] that states: "You shall not hand over a slave who has fled to you from his master. He shall dwell among you, in the place that he chooses within one of your gates, where it is good for him – do not wrong him".
>
> (TM 2018: 1)

By April 2018, TM had contributed to getting PM Netanyahu to rethink his policy, which meant that half of the Eritrean and Sudanese refugees would be resettled in Western nations through the auspices of the office of the United Nations High Commissioner for Refugees, and the other half were allowed to remain in Israel.

Conclusion

The example of TM's articulation of Jewish teachings and their work provides a counter-challenge to the exclusionist theology of Jewish religious extremists. TM presents a vision of Israel as a Jewish and democratic country where the rights of non-Jews are fully respected, upheld, and sustained by the state, government, judiciary, and the Jewish Orthodox religious establishment. Its work challenges these official bodies to uphold the commitment given to the Prophetic teachings of freedom, justice, and peace, which is part of the 1948 Declaration of the Establishment of Israel. Israel's non-Jewish citizens and Palestinians living in Israel and the Occupied Territories continue to face attacks regularly by Jewish religious extremists who seek to destroy their rights of identity, quality of life, and existence. So, can Israeli Jewish voices, like those of TM staff and volunteers, working to build Israel as an inclusive society succeed by drawing on the teachings, principles, and values of Judaism and models of liberal democracy to help create change in Israel? This question can be answered with cautious optimism. There are grounds for cautious optimism if the demands for change increase and intensify on the government, state, judiciary, and the Jewish Orthodox religious establishment to fulfil their responsibility to ensure that all the criteria of the international human rights regime, to which the state of Israel is a signatory, are met. This means that the state, government, and the Jewish Orthodox religious establishment take effective and robust measures to make the presence of Jewish extremist violence, aimed at destroying the rights of non-Jews, totally unacceptable in a Jewish and democratic state. And finally, the cautious optimism emerges also from the presence and work of TM and other such Israeli faith-based organizations which show that there remains a moral conscience in Israel concerning the essentiality of upholding human rights.

References

Babylonian Talmud (BTYeb). (500). (1938). *Tractate Yebamoth*. Translated by Israel W. Slotki. London: Soncino Press.

Brichto, Herbert Chanan. (1979). "The Hebrew Bible on Human Rights", in David Sidorsky (ed.). *Essays on Human Rights: Contemporary Issues and Jewish Perspectives*. Philadelphia: Jewish Publication Society of America, 215–233.

B'Tselem. (2020). *About B'Tselem*. Accessed from www.btselem.org/about_btselem [Date accessed October 20, 2021].

Israel Population Immigration and Border Authority (IPIBA). (2018). *Foreigners in Israel Data, First Quarter of 2018*. Accessed from www.gov.il/BlobFolder/generalpage/foreign_workers_stats/he/%D7%A8%D7%91%D7%A2%D7%95%D7%9F%201.pdf [Date accessed December 10, 2021].

Knesset. (1992). *Basic Law: Human Dignity and Liberty*. Accessed from www.knesset.gov.il/laws/special/eng/basic3_eng.htm [Date accessed October 20, 2021].

Maimonides, Moses. (1190). *Guide for the Perplexed*. Translated by M. Friedländer (1903). London: Routledge and Kegan Paul Ltd.

Maoz, Asher. (2004). "Can Judaism Serve as a Source of Human Rights?", *Heidelberg Journal of International Law* 64: 677–722.

Midrash (MDSif). (200). *Sifrei Devarim*. Translated by Rabbi Shraga Silverstein, n/d (unpublished). Accessed from www.sefari.org/Sifrei_Devarim.49?lang=bi [Date accessed October 20, 2021].

Novak, David. (1996). "Religious Human Rights in the Judaic Tradition", *Emory International Law Review* 69: 69–83.

Polish, Daniel F. (1982). "Judaism and Human Rights", in Arlene Swidler (ed.). *Human Rights in Religious Traditions*. New York: The Pilgrim Press, 40–50.

Rabbis for Human Rights (RHR). (2020). *Who Are We?* Accessed from www.rhr.org.il/eng [Date accessed December 15, 2021].

Shani, Ayelett. (2017). "Judaism Is Not a Murderous Religion: The Israeli Group That Stands Up to Jewish Terrorism", *Haaretz*, July 15, 2017.

Tag Meir. (2017). *Project Legal Work*. Accessed from www.tag-meir.org.il/en/project-legal-work/ [Date accessed December 14, 2021].

Tag Meir. (2018). *Letter to PM Netanyahu*. Accessed from www.tag-meir.org.il/en/rabbis-say-no-to-deportation-of-refugees/ [Date accessed December 14, 2021].

Tag Meir. (2019). *The Fifth Flower Parade of the Tag Meir Forum*. Accessed from www.tag-meir.org.il [Date accessed April 10, 2022].

Tag Meir. (2022a). "Israeli Settlers Pepper-spray Baby Near Westbank Outpost", *Facebook Post*, May 24, 2022. Accessed from www.facebook.com/tagmeirisrael/posts/5557229134310519 [Date accessed May 26, 2022].

Tag Meir. (2022b). "Tag Meir Flyer for Jerusalem Day", *Facebook Post*, June 1, 2022. Accessed from www.facebook.com/tagmeirisrael/photos/a.567063056660510/5578220855544680/ [Date accessed June 1, 2022].

Tag Meir. (n.d.). *About Us*. Accessed from www.tag-meir.org.il/en/ [Date accessed December 14, 2021].

4.4

CHRISTIAN PERSPECTIVE

Jesus Christ the Liberator

Friedrich Lohmann

Introduction

In the previous case study on the Christian perspective, two variations of the "traditionalistic" problem for the human rights idea (see Chapter 3.1) were outlined: the identification of a traditional, non-egalitarian morality with the requirements of a so-called natural order, as in the case of the current Russian Orthodox Church (ROC), and a focus on personal healing and salvation that justifies disregard of social change, as in the case of many branches of Pentecostalism. This disregard of social change in Pentecostalism is based on a certain image of Jesus Christ, as the personal healer and saviour. In this chapter, I will present a very different way of understanding the life and work of Jesus, as it is at the very heart of Christian liberation theology, thereby showing that Christian theology has great potential to support human rights claims, instead of undermining them, as in the ROC and some branches of Pentecostalism.

The part of Christian theology that reflects on Jesus Christ is called Christology. Given that he is the central person of Christian belief, it is evident that the respective Christology of a church has a strong bearing on its whole way to conceive of the Christian belief. Most churches commit to the Christological formula agreed upon at the Council of Chalcedon, back in 454 AD. It says that Jesus Christ has a divine and a human nature and that he is entirely divine as well as entirely human. It is, however, very difficult to conceive of a complete equilibrium between both natures and usually either the divine or the human side of Jesus Christ gets overemphasized. In the first case, theologians speak of a "high" Christology and in the second, it is a "low" Christology. For most of the history of the church, High Christologies were the preferred way to go. The divine characteristics of Jesus, like his power to heal and his life without sin, were emphasized, whereas specific human traits, like his suffering, were put rather aside. The Pentecostal Christology,

DOI: 10.4324/9781003344537-15

which was briefly presented in the previous chapter from the Christian perspective, is an example for such a High Christology: Christ is king, he has divine power, and he prepares the way for humanity to be reconciled with God, which is, in this perspective, by far his most important task.

However, this is not the only way to understand Jesus Christ. In the past decades, Low Christologies gained a lot of momentum. They are, among other current trends, an important part of theologies of liberation, which, for their part, have found support by theologians from around the globe since their inception in the 1960s. By examining the Christology that underlies different theologies of liberation, we can see how a new look on Jesus Christ offers new potential to embrace the human rights idea from a Christian perspective.

The low Christology of liberation theology

Theology of liberation is by far not homogenous. There are different emphases possible, for example, to understand which group of the population needs liberation. Still, there is a common trait of all liberation theologies: liberation is understood less spiritually – the personal liberation from sin – than socially, as the liberation from social, political, and economic oppression. Given that liberation is seen, with all Christian theology, as a work of God performed by Jesus Christ, this new understanding of liberation is echoed by a new understanding of Jesus Christ. This can be shown in all kinds of Christian liberation theology, and I will give some examples of the Christology connected with liberation theology.

Latin America was, arguably, the first region of global Christianity to develop a particular theology of liberation. It was also Latin American theologians who first devoted special attention to Christology from their new perspective. Leonardo Boff and Jon Sobrino wrote monographs dealing with Christology, in the conviction that the perception of Jesus Christ was key not only to distinguish their new theological approach from others but also to argue for its closeness to the Christian gospel itself.

We can start with a passage from Sobrino's work that points out the specific approach of liberation theology to Christology:

> Traditional soteriology, too, has contributed to this naïve and too readily reconciling vision of Christ by interpreting his cross as the transcendental reconciliation of God with human beings but outside the context of the historical conflict caused by historical human sins. Paradoxically, the cross has been used as a symbol for the greatest of conflicts and the greatest of sins on the cosmic and transcendental plane, but not to reflect the most serious conflicts and the historical sins that led Jesus to the cross and that today lead the crucified peoples there. The practical consequences of this have been to produce an image of Christ devoid of the real conflict of history and Jesus' stand on it, which has encouraged quietist or ultra-pacifist ideologies and support for anything going by the name "law and order".
>
> (Sobrino 1993: 16)

In addition to the clear-cut distinction from other, not the least Pentecostal, ways to understand the Christian gospel, two specific emphases of liberation theology and its Christology can be seen here: the emphasis on "real history" and the analogy made between the historical Jesus and the oppressed people of today. Like Jesus in his time, they are "crucified" today.

The first point is a common starting point in all Christian theologies of liberation. They contest any idea of salvation that does not include the given human society and its transformation:

> To work, to transform this world, is to become a man and to build the human community; it is also to save. Likewise, to struggle against misery and exploitation and to build a just society is already to be part of the saving action, which is moving towards its complete fulfillment.
>
> (Gutiérrez 1988: 91)

This interest in "this world" and its transformation is theologically justified by recurring first of all to ancient Israel and its struggles, with the exodus from Egypt as a founding story of liberation. Second, the theology of liberation dwells upon the fact that God took up human flesh and became a historical person. Further up, the life and message of this incarnate God, Jesus Christ, show a particular interest in marginalized people and their liberation from oppression.

> The spirit of the Lord has been given to me, for he has anointed me. He has sent me to bring the Good News to the poor, to proclaim liberty to captives and to the blind new sight, to set the downtrodden free, to proclaim the Lord's year of favor.
>
> (Luke 4: 18–19, as quoted in Boff 1980: 52)

These are, according to the Gospel of Luke, words from the first sermon of Jesus in Nazareth, and there is no statement from Christian liberation theology leaving out this sermon as a proof for Jesus's historical mission. The same emphasis is given to the fact that his deeds matched his words, by an attitude of non-discrimination against the marginalized groups of his society: "complete openness to God and others; indiscriminate love without limits" (Boff 1980: 97).

This mission is not over yet, which brings us to the second emphasis of a Christology of liberation mentioned earlier. Jesus, in his time, did not only preach in favour of the marginalized and encounter them in a non-discriminatory spirit. He furthermore shared their destiny when he was put to death for his message and punished with a particular cruel method of execution, applied only to people on the bottom of the social ladder. This is why Sobrino can call Jesus a "martyr for human rights" (cf. Sobrino 1992: 67). There is "a real parallel with the concrete situation of the believer here and now" (Sobrino 1978: 87), which makes the fact that Jesus was resurrected by God and thereby legitimized in his mission all the more important. If "the resurrection rehabilitated Jesus before the world" (Boff

1980: 129), all those who continue his struggle for the marginalized today are justified as well.

From Latin America, Christian liberation theology spread all over the globe. I'll give two examples for the global human rights activism inspired by this reading of the Christian gospel.

Black theology

I am first going to focus on the United States and black theology as an important variation of Christian liberation theology. Even if a specific "black" theology can be traced back historically to much earlier beginnings, the main voice to start the movement was James H. Cone in the late 1960s. Cone shares with other representatives of Christian liberation theology the focus on current social injustices, the active fight against them, and the intention to justify this fight theologically: "Theology [. . .] is the second step, a reflective action taken in response to the first act of a practical commitment in behalf of the poor" (Cone 1990: XIX). This theological reflection is based on a fresh look into the Bible and especially the story of Jesus. "Christian theology begins and ends with Jesus Christ" (Cone 1990: 110).

> Jesus Christ, therefore, in his humanity and divinity, is the point of departure for a black theologian's analysis of the meaning of liberation. There is no liberation independent of Jesus' past, present, and future coming. He is the ground of our present freedom to struggle and the source of our hope that the vision disclosed in our historical fight against oppression will be fully realized in God's future.
>
> (Cone 1997: 127)

The identification of the oppressed with Jesus as "God's suffering servants" (Cone 1997: 163) led some theologians of the movement to the vision of a "Black Christ", be it symbolically or even ethnically (Douglas 1994).

"The Black Christ" was, actually, the title of a poem published by Countee Cullen already in 1929, which ends with the following verses:

> How Calvary in Palestine,
> Extending down to me and mine,
> Was but the first leaf in a line
> Of trees on which a Man should swing
> World without end, in suffering
> For all men's healing, let me sing.
> (Cullen 1929: 69)

The leading idea of the poem is the same as in the later movement: by proposing a historical continuity between the crucifixion of Jesus at Calvary and the lynching of black people in the United States, Cullen imagined "Christ identify-ing with the contemporary marginalized victims of white supremacy" (Williams 2021: 66). This identification by God through Christ – and this means beyond the crucifixion also his incarnation, life, teaching, and resurrection – was felt to be a recognition of the struggle of black people in the United States for dignity and equality.

This brings us to the current Black Lives Matter (BLM) movement.

The BLM movement

The BLM movement is a complex phenomenon and so is its relationship with religion: some of its proponents emphasize the religious background of their strug-gle against racism, while others take a decisively secular standpoint (Cameron and Sinitiere 2021a; Lloyd 2018). It is, therefore, not the intention of the following remarks to claim a priority of religious, let alone Christian, ideas in BLM. Still, it seems to be worthwhile to ask for historical roots of the movement and to show how the Black theology of liberation, which was presented in the previous section, is an inspiration for BLM.

The first point to be mentioned here is the predominance of a structural and not personal understanding of human sin that black theology has in common with all types of Christian theology of liberation. This notion of sin prepares the way for the fight against structural racism in BLM (Miller 2020). The second point is the recognition of Black people as suffering servants of God, as it was illus-trated in the previous section. This idea of a fundamental recognition – against the actual, despised status of black people in society – is at the very heart of the BLM movement: Black lives "matter" and, therefore, their equal rights must be claimed. Already the initial Facebook post from Alicia Garza emphasizes this counterfactual recognition when it ends with the following words: "black people. I love you. I love us. Our lives matter" (as quoted in Lloyd 2018: 219). Later on, Garza elabo-rated on this point:

> Black Lives Matter is an ideological and political intervention in a world where Black lives are systematically and intentionally targeted for demise. It is an affirmation of Black folks' contributions to this society, our humanity, and our resilience in the face of deadly oppression.
>
> (Garza 2014)

"#BlackLivesMatter doesn't mean your life isn't important – it means that Black lives, which are seen as without value within White supremacy, are important to your liberation" (ibid.). In a jointly written post for Martin Luther King Day in 2015, the three founders of BLM reclaim the legacy of the 1960s civil rights move-ment: "Dr. King's dream tackled poverty and systemic inequality. Ultimately his vision was a society with human rights for all" (Tometi et al. 2015). This means, first of all, justice, dignity, and recognition for those at the margins of society. Opal

Tometi, the leading author of this post, identifies as a Christian: "I'm a believer, I believe in Jesus as a revolutionary person . . . that's my grounding" (as quoted in Cameron and Sinitiere 2021b: 2; Patrisse Cullors practises a West African Yoruba religious tradition known as Ifa, whereas Alicia Garza was raised in the Jewish tradition, cf. ibid.).

Dalit theology

Another example for the potentials of Christian ideas, and particularly Christology, for the advancement of human rights is Dalit theology, focused on the caste of the "untouchables", with its intent to support the "liberative process" (Massey 2014: 11) of the Dalit people in India by a new reading of the Christian gospel, showing that any discrimination is against its message: "For anyone who passively accepted such discrimination it would imply tacit complicity in a sinful structure and a contradiction of the examples set by Jesus" (Rajkumar 2010: 115). It is, once again, the Biblical Jesus who inspires the fight for equality and human rights. Jesus "teaches radical egalitarianism and brokerless relationships and thereby empowers Dalits to stand for their rights" (Jeremiah 2010: 162).

> Essentially, Jesus advocated human rights in order to restore the broken image of God by redeeming dignity and respect for all human beings. In the context of unjust and exploitative economics and politics, this Christological perspective becomes meaningful and pertinent to emulate.
>
> (Ibid.)

In this context, the theology of the Christian missionaries who brought Christianity to India is heavily criticized. Their theology neglected the structures of oppression in the Indian society because it was, in the footsteps of pietism, centred exclusively on the individual person, on "personal holiness" (Massey 2014: 88). In the eyes of today's Dalit theologians, this was the idea of a " 'half salvation'" (Massey 2014: 83) that has to be replaced by "whole salvation" (Massey 2014: 234), which is brought about not by social quietism or escapism but by a "spirituality of combat" (ibid.). As in so many other theologies of liberation, this new vision of Christianity and its task in society is based on the example of Jesus and especially his first sermon in Nazareth that "envisions the transformation of the whole human society" (Massey 2014: 209).

Dalit Christian activism for equality and human rights is directed against discrimination both in society and in the church (Ashok and Boopalan 2015). A current example is the struggle of the Dalit Christian Liberation Movement for equal representation within the hierarchy of the Catholic Church in India. In the broader sense of Dalit politics, the example of Lutheran Dalits in South India can be mentioned who feel empowered to claim their rights in society because of the active role they are entrusted with in their Christian congregations (Mocherla 2021: 121–122).

Conclusion

Despite its ambivalent history with regard to human rights, Christian theology offers a lot of support for the idea of equal rights for all human beings. This support stems from the very heart of Christianity, the person of Jesus Christ. The three examples of Christian theologies of liberation from different parts of the world (Latin America, United States, and India), which are referred to in this section, all have in common that they get their inspiration from a fresh reading of the Biblical gospel: Jesus was a predecessor of human rights activism and his mission continues in the human rights struggles of our time.

References

Ashok, Kumar M., and Sunder J. Boopalan. (2015). "Indian Christians in Conflict: Dalit Christian Movement in Contemporary India", in Stephen Hunt (ed.). *Handbook of Global Contemporary Christianity: Themes and Developments in Culture, Politics, and Society.* Leiden: Brill, 308–324.

Boff, Leonardo. (1980). *Jesus Christ Liberator: A Critical Christology for Our Time.* London: SPCK.

Cameron, Christopher, and Phillip Luke Sinitiere (eds.). (2021a). *Race, Religion, and Black Lives Matter: Essays on a Moment and a Movement.* Nashville, TN: Vanderbilt University Press.

Cameron, Christopher, and Phillip Luke Sinitiere. (2021b). "Introduction", in Christopher Cameron and Phillip Luke Sinitiere (eds.). *Race, Religion, and Black Lives Matter: Essays on a Moment and a Movement.* Nashville, TN: Vanderbilt University Press, 1–14.

Cone, James H. (1990). *A Black Theology of Liberation. Twentieth Anniversary Edition.* Maryknoll, NY: Orbis Books.

Cone, James H. (1997). *God of the Oppressed. Revised Edition.* Maryknoll, NY: Orbis Books.

Cullen, Countee. (1929). *The Black Christ & Other Poems.* New York/London: Harper & Brothers.

Douglas, Kelly Brown. (1994). *The Black Christ.* Maryknoll, NY: Orbis Books.

Garza, Alicia. (2014). *A Herstory of the #BlackLivesMatter Movement.* Accessed from https://thefeministwire.com/2014/10/blacklivesmatter-2/ [Date accessed November 13, 2022].

Gutiérrez, Gustavo. (1988). *A Theology of Liberation: History, Politics, and Salvation. Revised Edition with a New Introduction.* Maryknoll, NY: Orbis Books.

Jeremiah, Anderson H.M. (2010). "Exploring New Facets of Dalit Christology: Critical Interaction with J.D. Crossan's Portrayal of the Historical Jesus", in Sathianathan Clarke, Deenabandhu Manchala, and Philip Vinod Peacock (eds.). *Dalit Theology in the Twenty-first Century: Discordant Voices, Discerning Pathways.* Oxford/New York: Oxford University Press, 150–167.

Lloyd, Vincent. (2018). "How Religious is #BlackLivesMatter?", in Anthony B. Pinn (ed.). *Humanism and the Challenge of Difference.* Cham: Springer Nature, 215–237.

Massey, James. (2014). *Dalit Theology: History, Context, Text, and Whole Salvation.* New Delhi: Manohar.

Miller, Liam. (2020). "James Cone's Constructive Vision of Sin and the Black Lives Matter Movement", *Black Theology* 18 (1): 4–22.

Mocherla, Ashok Kumar. (2021). *Dalit Christians in South India: Caste, Ideology and Lived Religion.* London/New York: Routledge.

Rajkumar, Peniel. (2010). *Dalit Theology and Dalit Liberation: Problems, Paradigms and Possibilities*. Farnham/Burlington, VT: Ashgate.

Sobrino, Jon. (1978). *Christology at the Crossroads: A Latin American Approach*. Maryknoll, NY: Orbis Books. Second Printing.

Sobrino, Jon. (1992). *Theologie und Menschenrechte aus der Sicht der gekreuzigten Völker*. Graz: Verlag Jos A. Kienreich.

Sobrino, Jon. (1993). *Jesus the Liberator: A Historical-Theological Reading of Jesus of Nazareth*. Maryknoll, NY: Orbis Books.

Tometi, Opal, Alicia Garza, and Patrisse Cullors-Brignac. (2015). *Celebrating MLK Day: Reclaiming Our Movement Legacy*. Accessed from https://ayotometi.org/celebrating-mlk-day-reclaiming-our-movement-legacy/ [Date accessed November 13, 2022].

Williams, Reggie L. (2021). *Bonhoeffer's Black Jesus: Harlem Renaissance Theology and an Ethic of Resistance*. Revised Edition. Waco, TX: Baylor University Press.

4.5

ISLAMIC AND IRANIAN PERSPECTIVES ON HUMAN RIGHTS

Potentials

Katajun Amirpur and Ingrid Overbeck

In what follows, we will introduce three thinkers who are influencing public debates among Muslims worldwide, especially debates in the West, where all three have spent extended periods of time – Mohammad Shabestari, Abdolkarim Soroush, and Mohsen Kadivar. They all take Western influences, theories, and approaches and integrate them into an Islamic frame of reference by combining them with Islamic concepts.

The Iranian cleric Mohammad Shabestari (b. 1936) once pointedly said that the question is not whether Islam and human rights are compatible but whether contemporary Muslims want to allow this compatibility. He meant that there are more than enough theories and approaches that would make Islam and democracy, Islam and equality, and Islam and human rights compatible. But to be effective, they need to be applied and put into practice. His position is similar to that of American sociologists of religion who are advocating a global civil society and a global religion on the basis of shared values. Religions to his mind are the bearers of those global sacred values we wish to become universally accepted. He has formulated a new approach to Islamic revelation and works towards an acceptance of human rights not merely owed to circumstances but grounded in theology as an exponent of traditional religion.

In 1968, Shabestari accepted an invitation to head the Islamic Centre in Hamburg; he had been trained in Qom, the recognized centre for Iranian religious studies. Shabestari returned to Iran in 1977 and studied the Protestant theologians Paul Tillich and Karl Barth in depth, as well as the hermeneutic philosophy of Hans-Georg Gadamer. His reading was motivated primarily by the question of how Islam is compatible with democracy and human rights, that is, how Islamic teachings can be reconciled with the achievements of modernity. Shabestari's thoughts revolved around the following idea: an objective reading of texts is impossible. All readers are guided to some degree by the knowledge they bring to their reading.

DOI: 10.4324/9781003344537-16

From this, he draws a far-reaching conclusion: no reading of the Quran can claim to be the only correct one. In doing so, he largely follows lines of reasoning that originated with German hermeneuticists. As a doctrine of human understanding, hermeneutics must assume that the human capacity for understanding is limited. Therefore, it must insist on the historical contextualization of all human thought and knowledge. Shabestari applies this thought to the Quran, writing: "What has been formulated in a specific historical context requires a translation of its content and a reformulation to be understood in a different context" (Shabestari 1996: 14).

Modern hermeneutics teaches that the meaning of any text is a hidden truth that can only be revealed through interpretation. Only through this process, according to Shabestari, can a text be made to "speak". Without interpretation, neither text nor language can be intelligible: understanding must become an essentially never-ending conversation about the interpretation of historical and cultural heritage. He adopts Gadamer's idea that there can be no understanding that is free of all preconceptions, "[. . .] however much the will of our knowledge must be directed toward escaping their thrall" (Gadamer 2004: 484). Although there can be no understanding free from prejudice, the prejudices themselves must be subjected to constant scrutiny in the process of understanding.

Although he never mentions the Quran by name, it is clear that this is precisely what he means when he explains the hermeneutic principle, which states that the more centuries there are between the creation of a text and its reading, the more difficult it becomes to interpret it. Readers who live in a time and have experiences radically different from those of the author must translate the text into their own horizons. By this, he means that the Quran must be contextualized. Shabestari aims to understand the historical situation in which the text was created, what the author wanted to convey to the audience, what linguistic gifts and skills were available to him, and under what historical conditions his addressees lived. These questions can only be answered through a thorough historical analysis. Shabestari said any other approach would only lead to the "interpreter" imposing his own biases on the text (cf. Shabestari 1996: 19). For Shabestari, people cannot be "blank slates". He argues that biases and guiding interests are universal features of reading and, therefore, there is a multiplicity of possible interpretations. For this reason, he sees legalistic Islam, which focuses on the legal aspects of the faith, as only one possible interpretation among many, however much it may claim to be the only legitimate one. It cannot be considered absolute and has no legitimate claim to be in accordance with the will of God.

He rejects "legalistic Islam" which he distinguishes from both spiritual Islam and traditional, quietist Islam. It is incompatible with democracy and human rights because it seeks to impose Quranic criminal law and a purportedly Quranic interpretation of human rights. For Shabestari, however, it is not Islamic law but faith that is at the heart of the religion. Accordingly, he does not see adherence to legal norms as central to an Islamic life but rather the inner spiritual attitude. True faith cannot be strengthened by forcing people to follow legalistic rules. Instead, he argues that the basis of all true faith is freedom of thought and free will.

But what must the political system look like in which Muslims can live their faith freely? Shabestari concludes from his Quranic hermeneutics that the Quran itself contains very few instructions for political rule. It only requires that government be just, nothing more. He backs up this assertion by pointing out that Ali ibn Abi Talib (600–661), the fourth caliph, merely instructed his governor in Egypt to rule justly and to respect the traditions of all the people in the newly conquered land. The fundamental question must be what system of government will allow the faith to be best realized:

> It follows from the logic of faith that the faithful must demand the establishment of a political and social order [. . .] in which they are better able to practice their faith freely and knowledgably. [. . .] Such a society will surely not be an oppressive or totalitarian one.
>
> (Shabestari 1997: 79)

He proposes a democratic system that gives its citizens full freedom because "faith is not an ideology". Such a system would allow people to best put human rights into practice.

Another world-leading contemporary Muslim intellectual is Abdulkarim Soroush (b. 1945). Soroush applied Western methods in his research and examined the diversity of Quranic interpretation from an epistemological perspective. Soroush was for a time one of the Iranian regime's most important ideologues, but his criticism of the ruling clergy and his claim to exclusivity in religious interpretation led to his fall from grace in 1996. In response to his article "Freedom and Clergy", he was first attacked in the media, then threatened with death and was physically assaulted (Soroush 1995a: 24). In it, Soroush argued that public funding had transformed the clergy into a social interest group that claimed a monopoly to defend its privilege, and that this claim to exclusive insight led to the ossification of religious thought. He wrote: "Any group that sees itself as the bearer of the only valid interpretation of religion and seeks to base political power and material advantage on that claim must be rejected" (Soroush 1995b: 26). This was tough stuff in a theocratic state. Soroush initially stayed abroad only sporadically, officially in his capacity as a visiting professor. For the past 20 years, he has lived in permanent exile. His scholarly work took him to such prestigious institutions as the Wissenschaftskolleg in Berlin, Harvard, Princeton, and Yale.

The central tenet of Soroush's position is that religious knowledge is mutable. Just as all human knowledge changes with time and the state of science, the same must be true of human knowledge about religion. Over time, new interpretations of faith emerge according to the conditions under which the interpreters themselves live.

Soroush's epistemological point, then, is that it is possible to expand understanding infinitely, but that such expansion is always only an approximation of the object. Ordinary people can never really know what God expects of them. They can never understand what the divine law really is or what it intends. God's intentions are inscrutable, and all alleged knowledge of them, echoing Karl Popper, is mere presumption. Epistemology teaches him that human understanding of the Quran can never fully grasp the text itself and its true intentions. Human understanding of the Quran, like all human understanding, depends on the circumstances of its time.

For Soroush, human rights are simply the dictates of human reason. It is, therefore, *ipso facto* impossible for them to contradict religion because God's will cannot be against reason. The fact that they originated in a context outside religion does not prevent Soroush from considering their realization possible and even necessary in an Islamic system. The rights of God would remain inviolable and human and divine values would be in full harmony. He takes a position here that is rarely found outside secular circles; like them, he assumes that human beings, by virtue of their humanity alone, have rights that derive from outside the sphere of religion. Unlike the secularists, however, he takes this position from a religious standpoint.

Based on this premise, Soroush attempts to develop a blueprint for a political system that is both Islamic and democratic: a religious-democratic government. A religious democracy earns its designation in enabling believers to live religious lives. A religious society is not a society that applies religious laws, but one whose members voluntarily profess religion. His ideal state is religious in that it is governed by faith, not in a formal legislative or judicial capacity but as a spirit that permeates all aspects of the state. Soroush advocates democracy as a solution because it is the system of government best suited to protect religion, that is, the rights of God. It protects religion from being dismissed by its supposed spokesmen from the will of God. Where human rights are respected, religion is safe from such abuses. For this reason, Soroush sees the ideal form of government as both democratic and truly religious.

Soroush seeks to adapt his understanding of religion to the modern understanding of human rights, not the other way around. He could rightly be called a post-Islamist intellectual: For Soroush, human rights are not religious; they are acceptable to any truly religious person, apart from being obviously necessary. Yet, despite this near-complete formal identity, there remains a crucial difference from the Western idea of democracy: Soroush's religious-democratic state is directed towards a divine goal, the search for a just society is a divine calling that God's will requires.

The third intellectual is Mohsen Kadivar (b. 1959), who was introduced in Chapter 3.5. Kadivar's central statement, which undoubtedly identifies him as a post-Islamic intellectual, can be summarized as follows: people might expect religion to provide them with general principles and values to guide their lives, but practical concerns fall more into the realm of "human experience" – a veiled reference to secular norms. Thus, Kadivar argues that different historical periods require different political and economic systems.

Kadivar's publications are primarily concerned with the compatibility of Islam and human rights. He bases his argument for the compatibility of Islam and human rights on a hermeneutical reading of the Quran. In a lecture on "Freedom of Thought and Religion", he argues that there is an interpretation based on the original sources of Islam that is consistent with freedom of religion or belief as enshrined in the Universal Declaration of Human Rights. Its proponents are usually referred to as Muslim innovators, reformists, or religious enlightenment advocates. Kadivar lists the main features of reformist or spiritual Islam as follows (cf. Kadivar 2006: 119–142).

All members of society and every individual, without distinction of religion, sex, race or creed, have a share in determining their political destiny, in shaping their common public sphere, and all enjoy equal rights. On this basis, no distinction can be made between the different schools of Islamic jurisprudence, between Muslims and non-Muslims, or between men and women – either in terms of the right to vote or to stand for election, or in terms of their right to participate in public life.

Freedom of religion and belief means an individual's right to freely choose any and all ideologies and religions he likes. It also means the freedom and the right to think, to have beliefs and values, to express one's religion and opinions, to partake in religious rites and practices, and to freely reach religious values to one's children and to coreligionists. [. . .] Freedom of religion means doing all these freely so long as others' rights and liberties are not infringed upon, and public order and morality are not disturbed.

The basic religious texts of Islam – the Quran and the Sunnah – contain both teachings that are unchanging, regardless of time and place, and teachings that are changeable and bound to the conditions of their time. These teachings were transmitted in relation to the conditions prevailing at the time and lose their validity or relevance when those conditions change.

For Kadivar, the question concerns what form of Islam people will choose. He writes:

Islam is limpid as rain and, as it flows over the bed of history and various lands, takes on the hue, taste, and odor of various customs, although of course most of this is from the time and place of the Age of the Revelation.
(Kadivar 2011: 460)

Here, Kadivar is in complete agreement with Shabestari: it is the Muslims who decide. The question is not regarding what Islam is. Anything can be justified or read into it from the Quran, depending, as Shabestari pointed out, on one's own prejudices and interests. One finds not only democracy, equality, and human rights in the Quran but also patriarchy, socialism, or theocracy. Or to put it in the words of the fourth caliph, Ali:

"The Quran is nothing but a scripture between two covers. It cannot speak. It is the people who speak to it" (Abi Talib 1972: 386).

Final remarks

The question of whether Islam is compatible with human rights must be answered in a differentiated manner. It is by no means Islam in itself that causes difficulties in the reception of human rights but at best a certain understanding of Islam that results from the respective Islamic conception of law. For reformist Islam thinkers, the defence of human rights is reasonable and consistent with the Islamic precept of justice. They are encouraged by the fact that logic and philosophy have been similarly criticized throughout the history of Islam. The phrase "he who applies logic becomes a heretic" took centuries to clarify that formal logic has nothing to do with idolatry. Recognition of human rights is not a capitulation to the West but a capitulation to the way of reasonable people (*sira al-'uqala*) and justice.

How will the Islamic world deal with the presented approaches of the so-called reformist Islam? Will they be considered legitimate enough to still be accepted as authentically Islamic? Crucial for the enforcement of human rights is the identification of people with the preconditions that establish human rights as a moral claim. In order to live up to Islam's universalist claim, Muslims must find ways to make their assertions about what is right and good accessible to others, non-believers, and people of other faiths, by legitimizing human rights in a way that is understandable to all people.

References

Abi Talib, 'Ali ibn. (1972). *Nahj al-balagha*. Tehran: 'Ali Naqi Feiz ol-Eslam.

Gadamer, Hans-Georg. (2004). *Truth and Method*. London: Continuum.

Kadivar, Mohsen. (2006). "Freedom of Religion and Belief in Islam", in Mehran Kamrava (ed.). *The New Voices of Islam. Rethinking Politics and Modernity*. Berkeley: University of California Press, 119–142.

Kadivar, Mohsen. (2011). "From Traditional Islam to Islam as an End in Itself", *Die Welt des Islams* 51: 459–484.

Shabestari, Mohammad. (1996). *Hermenutik, ketāb va sonnat*. Tehran: Tahr-e nou.

Shabestari, Mohammad. (1997). *Īmān va āzādī*. Tehran: Tahr-e nou.

Soroush, Abdolkarim. (1995a). "Ḥurrīyyat va rouḥānīyyat", *Kiyan* 24 (5): 2–11.

Soroush, Abdolkarim. (1995b). "Saqf-I ma'īshat bar sutūn-i sharī'at", *Kiyan* 26 (5): 26.

PART V

Now What? Implications and Recommendations

5

NOW WHAT? RECOMMENDATIONS FOR BUILDING COOPERATION BETWEEN SECULAR AND RELIGIOUS ACTORS

Pauline Kollontai and Friedrich Lohmann

Introduction

In writing this book, our overall aim was to identify and discuss the significance of religion in the context of human rights concerning the role religion can play either in undermining and not supporting human rights or in the way it supports and promotes these rights. In this volume, we speak from within our respective religious traditions. While self-critically analysing what we perceive as shortcomings and hermeneutical deficits, we have identified and examined the resources, approaches, and methods within each of our religious traditions that can promote and help secure human rights using case studies set in four different geographical contexts, thereby providing "real life" contexts for the discussion. In this final chapter, we present four recommendations for developing and enhancing cooperation between secular and religious actors.

The engagement of religious actors with human rights has grown theoretically through statements, declarations, discourses, and a variety of practical activities over the past few decades. The theoretical and case study chapters presented in this book show that religion can be a constructive player in promoting and actively supporting human rights. However, the tendency is that religious actors are more likely to operate within faith-based networks and often have minimal engagement with policymakers, officials, and practitioners. Therefore, the reality of religious voices being isolated, minimized, or ignored by secular actors remains an issue. Several key questions need to be asked about why this happens. Is this a result of religious actors making a conscious decision not to engage with secular actors because they believe that a purely anthropocentric approach to human rights is insufficient? Is it because some religious actors consider that promoting equality of rights for all irrespective of gender, race, ethnicity, and sexual orientation is not in accordance with their interpretation of divine revelation? Is it the result of a dominant view

DOI: 10.4324/9781003344537-18

present among secular actors for centuries that religion is often the cause of wars and violence, of inequalities and division, and therefore not engaging religious actors in a whole host of issues concerning peace, justice, liberty, and rights is the preferred course of action? Do religious actors feel that their views and contributions are not listened to seriously because their beliefs and traditions are sometimes misunderstood or viewed as "out-of-date" and therefore having little relevance for contemporary societies? While the overtly negative and uninformed view of religion needs to be consciously addressed and corrected among secular actors, religious actors also must ask themselves if they can act responsibly and with integrity in the public sphere. Asking and addressing these questions is essential to the task at hand of developing and enhancing frameworks and spaces of engagement where religious and secular actors can work together in a culture of constructive and respectful cooperation on human rights protection, advocacy, and enforcement.

Recent progress on integrating religious actors

There has been a concerted effort on the part of some international and regional governmental organizations such as the United Nations (UN), the Organization for Security and Cooperation in Europe, the Council of Europe, the African Union, the Association of Southeast Asian Nations, the Organization of American State, the World Health Organization, and the World Bank to engage religious actors in some aspects of their discussions and work. These include issues such as building inclusive societies, strengthening democratic institutions, genocide prevention, the 2030 Sustainable Development Goals, climate change and environmental activism, and HIV/AIDS. A specific example of recognizing the importance of religious actors in promoting human rights and challenging those who violate such rights is seen in the work of the UN's Office of the High Commissioner for Human Rights (UNOHCHR). In 2012, after two years of regional workshops in Europe, Africa, Asia-Pacific, and the Americas with a range of experts and representatives, UNOHCHR issued the Rabat Plan of Action on the prohibition of incitement to national, racial, or religious hatred, which "emphasizes the role of politicians and religious leaders in preventing and speaking out against intolerance, discriminatory stereotyping and instances of hate speech" (UNOHCHR 2020: 1). In 2017, from meetings between faith-based and civil society actors under the auspices of UNOHCHR in Beirut, the Beirut Declaration on Faith for Rights (BDFR) was produced which included a Faith for Rights framework of values and actions. The opening statement said that religious actors have a significant role to play in human rights work and that cross-sector cooperation is essential:

> We, faith-based and civil society actors working in the field of human rights express our deep conviction that our respective religions and beliefs share a common commitment to upholding the dignity and the equal worth of all human beings. Shared human values and equal dignity are, therefore, common roots of our cultures. Faith and rights should be mutually reinforcing

spheres. Similarly, human rights can benefit from deeply rooted ethical and spiritual foundations provided by religion or beliefs.

(BDFR 2017: 1)

Two years later, in 2019, Veronica Michelle Bachelet, the UN High Commissioner for Human Rights, in her statement at the Global Summit on Religion and Peace, reiterated the importance of governments, religious authorities, and civil society actors working together:

> Religious leaders play a crucial role in either defending human rights, peace and security – or, unfortunately, in undermining them. Supporting the positive contributions of faith-based actors is crucial, as is preventing the exploitation of religious faith as a tool in conflicts, or as interpreted to deny people's rights. Human rights and faith can be mutually supportive.
>
> (Bachelet 2019: 1)

A further development from the 2017 BDFR was launching the #Faith4Rights toolkit online, translating the "Faith for Rights" framework into practical peer-to-peer learning and capacity-building programmes.

At the national government level, there has been some mirroring of these international and regional initiatives. In Germany, the government has been working to engage its religious communities on the issue of implementing the UN's Sustainable Development Goals. Since 2015, Muslim Imams, theologians, and other intellectual thinkers have been part of the Belgian government's deradicalization policy in Muslim communities. Several initiatives in the United States since 2000 have aimed to engage more formally and systematically with religious communities. For example, in 2002, the Agency for International Development focused on the role of religious actors in international development; in 2014, the government engaged with religious actors on aspects of foreign policy, including peacebuilding, development, and human rights, and in 2013 it established a dedicated Office of Religion and Global Affairs at the Department of State. Since 2021, the Biden administration has publicly recognized and has actively pursued a policy of engaging and working with religious communities in their faith-based approaches to overcoming COVID vaccine hesitancy. In Uganda, between 2007 and 2012, women from various religious communities worked with local government authorities to provide and improve health and care services for people living with HIV/AIDS and their family members in towns and villages; to review the educational policies concerning orphans and vulnerable children having access to Primary Education and to support the development of local economic services through setting up of village loan associations and micro-finance initiatives in villages.

All these examples demonstrate that religion has begun to be seen more by secular actors at national, regional, and international levels as having essential contributions to make. However, as Arsheim points out, "The interrelationship between religion and international organizations is marked by the commonality of ad hoc approaches, due largely to the widely held view that religions are residual and superfluous phenomena in late modern international society", and this can also be said of interrelationships between religious and secular actors at regional and national levels (Arsheim 2016: 502). While this landscape of recognition of religion has grown, there continue to be difficulties concerning the level and nature at which religious actors are included in decisions being made by secular actors. This raises the need to consider the overarching issue of what it means to have religious actors as equal partners, thereby ensuring better and equal integration of religious actors (individuals, congregations, institutions, FBOs) in human rights discussions and work.

Recommendation 1: religious literacy for secular actors

Religious literacy should be available to a range of actors from the community and local leaders to government leaders, policymakers, and practitioners. The importance of religious literacy is described as contributing to building "bridges of understanding and the capacity to think critically and contextually" (Mandaville and Nozell 2017: 6). It can help secular actors "identify access points within a religious community or understand the different roles of various religious figures and how their relationship could affect community dynamics" (ibid.). The recognition that religious actors do need to be consulted on issues such as those mentioned in earlier examples would suggest that awareness of the need for religious literacy among policymakers and practitioners has grown to some extent. The type of religious literacy available to policymakers and practitioners appears to be often provided through short, didactic workshops and courses. These are valuable in that a general introduction is provided to the beliefs and practices of religions and associated cultural factors with some application to specific issues within wider societies. One of the key reasons for short course delivery is the issue of time of those attending and sometimes financial costs for their respective institutions and organizations. However, with this type of delivery model, there is a danger that the diversity of beliefs and practices of religion, the fluidity of religion, and its geopolitical contextualization are not fully presented and can thereby minimize understanding. Also, religious concepts and narratives may not be sufficiently understood and engaged with (Davie 2012, 2013). The more substantive provision of religious literacy identified by Susan Hayward involves three levels:

1   Substantive Literacy: Understanding the teachings, doctrines, symbols, and practices of a religious tradition. This dimension seeks to genuinely understand a tradition through the eyes of the believer, sometimes referred to as the "insider" perspective.
2   Functional Literacy: Understanding the cultural, historical, political, and social contexts in which a particular religious tradition exists. This dimension seeks to take a broader view of a tradition – the "observatory" perspective.

3   Engagement Literacy: Understanding how and when to engage with religious actors. This dimension considers the ethical, legal, and strategic constraints on religious engagement that are relevant to peacebuilding – the "mindful" perspective (Hayward n.d.: 1–2).

These three levels provide a fuller understanding of religions and are more likely to safeguard secular actors against misinformed interpretations of the values and motives of religious communities, whether within national borders, regionally, or transnationally. Having an informed and comprehensive understanding of religions means "it is imperative that world leaders, policymakers, and practitioners prioritize their understanding of religion and the central role it plays in human affairs" (USIP n.d.:1).

Recommendation 2: "being equal partners" – organizational approach, principles, and values

Regarding their engagement with religious actors, secular actors require regular updating of their knowledge and understanding of a religious landscape within a specific country or regional or international context. They need to show a serious, consistent, and genuine interest in recognizing the importance of having religious actors involved in areas of their discussions and work. Also, it is essential to recognize that religious actors can provide insights and understanding of issues within the wider public sphere, as seen in the case studies presented in this book. Part of this approach requires secular actors to have regular and ongoing engagement with religious actors from the beginning or at least very early in discussions and decision-making processes before decisions are made and policies are drafted. Not doing so may render policies less effective in terms of their suitability and sustainability.

Stemming from this overall approach, four fundamental principles need to be demonstrated by secular actors. First, if religious actors are included in dialogue (talking and practically working together), secular partners must ensure that transparency and respect are demonstrated even when tensions and disagreements arise. Of course, this principle also needs to be adhered to by religious actors. Second, a common language and shared values must be identified to enable constructive and creative outcomes. Three and four are the concepts and practice of multipolarity (the interaction and independence of various actors) and transversality (secular and religious actors are willing to be involved in cross-sector dialogue) are needed to ensure that religious actors feel that they are equal partners (McDonagh et al. 2021: 138). Enabling religious actors to feel they are equal partners means ensuring they are not just included as "religious voices" but are genuinely listened to.

A final point in this section needs to be made about which religious actors to engage and work with. Typically, secular actors gravitate towards religious leaders because they are considered credible voices and theologically knowledgeable.

There is an overall danger in only ever engaging with religious leaders as Mandaville and Nozell point out in their work on working with religious leaders in countering violent extremism, "Too often, *credible voices* end up being code for religious figures who articulate views that are aligned with official government policy, or who refrain from directly criticizing political leaders" (Mandaville and Nozell 2017: 8). Another issue to take into consideration is that the leaders of religious authorities and institutions (e.g. Archbishop, Pope, Chief Rabbi, Lama) and among those who minister to local religious communities (e.g. Rabbis, Imams, Priests, Ministers, Vajrācārya) in many geopolitical contexts are usually men who may not always reflect or sufficiently represent the diversity of the religious landscape regarding the views, knowledge, and experiences, for example, of women, youth, ethnic minorities, and LGBTQ+. Also, it is important to avoid the tendency to only engage with representatives from the Abrahamic religions. Efforts should be made to include other religions such as Hinduism, Buddhism, Sikhism, Taoism, and native Indigenous religions. In addition, representatives of faith-based non-governmental organizations need to be included where relevant because they can offer insights as practitioners. Ensuring that the engagement and work with religious actors reflect this diversity as much as possible is essential to producing relevant and meaningful discussions, decisions, and policies.

The approach and organizational principles and values of secular actors in engaging and working with religious actors should aim to improve communication, build trust, and demonstrate that religion is taken seriously. This requires an approach "that does not consider religions to be anachronistic remnants of a distant past, as dangerous forces to be contained" or as always wanting to undermine or frustrate the work of secular actors (Arsheim 2016: 502). Secular actors need to work harder at overcoming the still dominant view that religion is often not compatible with democracy, and that religion is divisive. Based on this view the "logical" conclusion is to keep religion away from the work and policies of governments and regional and international organizations. To challenge this mindset, there are examples given in this book from four religious traditions. Numerous other examples can be seen worldwide that confirm that religion has an essential role through its resources and networks to positively contribute to public and political discourses. In other words, religion can make effective and often creative contributions to the work of secular actors (Banchoff and Wuthnow 2011).

Recommendation 3: recognition of the legitimacy, influence, knowledge, understanding, and experience of religious actors

The critical question often heard from secular actors is why they should engage and consult with religious actors concerning matters in wider society. This question arises from the scepticism remaining about whether religion can make any valuable contribution to the issues which seek to improve human existence and well-being, those issues which, for example, are identified in the UN's 17 Sustainable Development Goals. This scepticism is, to some extent, understandable, given the ambivalent nature of religion evidenced throughout the centuries, with religious actors articulating and promoting within their religious establishments and in wider society teachings and values that either promote human rights, peace, and justice or seek to oppose these. This ambivalent nature has been well evidenced in this book. In helping overcome these sceptical attitudes, religious actors have teachings, knowledge, and influence that can be used negatively or constructively within their religious communities and organizations, and which can extend across intra- and inter-religious borders. Religious actors, like their secular counterparts, must be willing to engage honestly and respectfully, particularly when disagreements and tensions arise because of religious sensitivities rooted in centuries of religious teachings that clash with secular ideas and sometimes with the teachings across religions.

Returning to the question of why secular actors should engage with religious actors, our response identifies three key reasons for this engagement that need to be recognized by secular actors. First, religious actors are seen among their religious followers as having legitimacy in articulating and formulating values and concepts according to religious teaching that shapes, influences, and determines how people of faith live their lives and relate to broader societal and global issues. Working alongside religious actors is the first step in recognizing that religious actors are seen by the followers as repositories of divinely inspired values, principles, and wisdom that they have the right to interpret and teach. The legitimacy factor leads to the second reason that the religious actor can be an influencer in either reinforcing, challenging, modifying or changing the opinions and actions of those within their faith communities. This is the second step in the recognition process, based on the assumption that religious actors can educate their followers to think and behave in ways that demonstrate respect and the importance of dignity and rights for all. The third reason is religious actors have the knowledge, understanding, and experience of a specific geographical context regarding the lived experiences and perspectives, especially of their own religious communities, sometimes of other religious communities, and more generally of people in wider society. This knowledge, understanding, and experience can be valuable in enabling secular actors to engage with the reality of the experience of people, religious or non-religious, when discussing and designing policies and strategies. Religious actors can provide invaluable insights into why there may be some resistance among some religious communities because of strongly held religious views and sensitivities that see secular policies and agendas as conflicting with religious beliefs. Such insights can contribute to finding ways of working to reduce or alleviate these differences and concerns. This is the third step in the recognition process; religious actors have "insider" knowledge and understanding that can assist secular actors in making better-informed decisions when designing and implementing policies and strategies.

Recommendation 4: religious actors promoting constructive partnership engagement and counteracting opposition within religions

Our book shows there are religious actors who either work independently or on an intra-religious or inter-religious basis and this sometimes involves engaging with secular actors. However, what also is presented in our book is that there are religious actors who either do not support human rights or are particular about the rights that they choose to support. Examples of rights sometimes not supported are gender justice and equality, LGBTQ+, and minority rights. While this chapter identifies a good deal of issues that secular actors need to continue to address, we present here recommendations that religious actors need to address concerning two issues. The first issue is what religious actors need to do to help create meaningful and sustainable religious and secular partnerships. The second is what more needs to be done by religious actors to challenge those within religions who are either against or indifferent to human rights.

Concerning the first issue, religious actors who are involved with secular partnerships need to ensure, like their secular partners, that their participation is transparent and respectful even when tensions and disagreements arise. This involves learning to understand the perspectives of secular actors and why they aim to adopt a particular position. However, the role of religious actors is not to be passive, thereby remaining on the periphery and being hesitant in not expressing their concerns to secular partners. It is also important that religious actors show that constructive engagement with secular partners is feasible and how to demonstrate this is presented in the opening statement of the "18 commitments on Faith for Rights" in the BDFR:

> As religions are necessarily subject to human interpretations, we commit to promote constructive engagement on the understanding of religious texts. Consequently, critical thinking and debate on religious matters should not only be tolerated but rather encouraged as a requirement for enlightened religious interpretations in a globalized world composed of increasingly multi-cultural and multi-religious societies that are constantly facing evolving challenges.
>
> (BDFR 2017a: 1)

Undertaking this commitment means that religious actors can clearly articulate to their secular partners "between the spiritual message of systems of faith, and religious rhetoric" and show that religions are diverse and dynamic and are not a static phenomenon (UNIA 2008: 17).

The second issue of how religious insiders can promote support for human rights within their institutions and communities is evidenced in this book, especially in the case studies which show that religious insiders are doing this with varying degrees of success. These examples demonstrate what has been identified by the authors of the

BDFR, and in their #Faith4Rights toolkit, as an overall commitment "to leverage the spiritual and moral weight of religions and beliefs with the aim of strengthening the protection of universal human rights and developing preventative strategies that we adapt to our local contexts" (BDFR 2017a: 4). Ibrahim Salama and Michael Wiener's book *Reconciling Religion and Human Rights* discusses the content and implementation of the "18 commitments on Faith for Rights". They argue that reconciling religion and human rights is possible and "Optimizing human rights protection, in practice, requires the full involvement of all influential non-State actors", including faith-based actors (Salama and Wiener 2022: 9).

Our case studies show how religious actors can counteract and challenge those within their own religious institutions and communities who oppose or are indifferent to human rights, (or specific areas of human rights), or themselves are involved in supporting human rights violations.

There are four key areas of activities for religious actors to do this. First, there is the advocacy of the importance of human rights within religious institutions and communities. This can be done, for example, through exhibitions, dialogue events, public and social media, and events such as vigils. The second is the task of publicly challenging and denouncing religious actors who violate human rights or are coalescing with secular actors who commit violations. Third is the work of reforming and refining religious education and training for laity delivered within religious institutions, including faith-based schools, in terms of making available teaching materials and books that challenge various expressions of prejudice and distrust which form the basis for opposing human rights. Fourth is the importance of sustaining religious actors who are favourable to human rights and help enhance their work in religious institutions and communities. This can be done by establishing inter- and intra-religious partnerships as well as with academics and academic organizations that specialize in religion and rights. These partnerships can be beneficial for the exchange of knowledge, understanding, skills, training, and good practice, all essential for providing moral support and for building capacity and sustainability for religious actors and their work.

Conclusion

The capacity and ability of religion to assist in advocating, improving, and helping in sustaining human rights work and the culture of dignity and respect which underpins this work are shown in this book. Ignoring this reality would be a missed opportunity for governments and regional and international bodies in their struggles against the ongoing indifference and violation of rights that continue to exist. Religion as a phenomenon is one of the oldest expressions of human thought and belief. Just over 85 per cent of the world's population identifies with a religion (WPR 2022: 1). The influence of religious actors supporting and advocating human rights to their own constituencies and beyond is a significant reality. For the reasons given earlier, their presence must be included in the discussions, decision-making spaces, and processes of secular actors.

References

Arsheim, Helge. (2016). "Religion and International Organizations", in Ian Hurd, Ian Johnstone, and Jacob Katz Cogan (eds.). *The Oxford Handbook of International Organizations*. Oxford: Oxford University Press, 490–507.

Bachelet, Veronica Michelle. (2019). *Promoting the Non-Discrimination and Protection of Human Rights of Religious Minorities, Refugees and Migrants in Ultra-Nationalist Contexts*. Accessed from www.ohchr.org/en/statements/2019/04/global-summit-religion-peace-and-security?LangID=E&NewsID=24531 [Date accessed July 10, 2022].

Banchoff, Thomas, and Robert Wuthnow (eds.). (2011). *Religion and the Global Politics of Human Rights*. Oxford/New York: Oxford University Press.

Beirut Declaration on Faith for Rights (BDFR). (2017). Accessed from www.ohchr.org/sites/default/files/BeirutDeclarationonFaithforRights.pdf [Date accessed July 26, 2022].

Beirut Declaration on Faith for Rights (BDFR). (2017a). *18 Commitments on Faith for Rights*. Accessed from www.ohchr.org/sites/default/files/Documents/Press/21451/18CommitmentsonFaithforRights.pdf [Date accessed July 26, 2022].

Davie, Grace. (2012). "Belief and Unbelief: Two Sides of a Coin", *Approaching Religion* 2 (1): 3–7.

Davie, Grace. (2013). *The Sociology of Religion: A Critical Review*. London: Sage.

Hayward, Susan. (n.d.). "Dimension of Religious Literacy", USIP Briefing. New York: USIP.

Mandaville, Peter, and Melissa Nozell. (2017). "Engaging Religion and Religious Actors in Countering Violent Extremism", Briefing Paper. ETH Zurich: Centre for Security Studies.

McDonagh, Philip, Kishan Manocha, John Neary, and Lucia Vazquez Mendoza. (2021). *On the Significance of Religion for Global Diplomacy*. London: Routledge.

Salama, Ibrahim, and Michael Wiener. (2022). *Reconciling Religion and Human Rights: Faith in Multilateralism*. Cheltenham/Northampton, MA: Edward Elgar Publishing.

United Nations Inter-Agency (UNIA). (2008). *Proceedings Report: United Nations Inter-agency Consultation on Engagement with Faith-based Organizations*. Accessed from www.unfpa.org/sites/default/files/resource-pdf/proceedings_fbo.pdf [Date accessed July 30, 2023].

United Nations Office of the High Commissioner for Human Rights (UNOHCHR). (2020). *OHCHR and the Faith of Rights Framework*. Accessed from www.ohchr.org/en/faith-for-rights [Date accessed July 24, 2022].

United States Institute of Peace. (n.d.). *Religious Literacy and Peacebuilding*. Accessed from www.usip.org/programs/religious-literacy-and-peacebuilding [Date accessed July 10, 2022].

World Population Review (WPR). (2022). *Religion by Country 2022*. Accessed from https://worldpopulationreview.com/country-rankings/religion-by-country [Date accessed July 27, 2022].

INDEX